MW00810091

Probability:
A Philosophical Introduction

'A fascinating philosophical tour of probability theory by a distinguished, insightful, and lucid guide.'

Alan Hájek, Australian National University

Probability: A Philosophical Introduction introduces and explains the principal concepts and applications of probability. It is intended for philosophers and others who want to understand probability as we all apply it in our working and everyday lives. The book is not a course in mathematical probability, of which it uses only the simplest results, and avoids all needless technicality.

The role of probability in modern theories of knowledge, inference, induction, causation, laws of nature, action and decision-making makes an understanding of it especially important to philosophers and students of philosophy, to whom this book will be invaluable both as a textbook and a work of reference.

In this book D. H. Mellor discusses the three basic kinds of probability – physical, epistemic, and subjective – and introduces and assesses the main theories and interpretations of them. The topics and concepts covered include

- chance
- frequency
- possibility
- propensity
- credence
- confirmation
- Bayesianism

Probability: A Philosophical Introduction is essential reading for all philosophy students and others who encounter or need to apply ideas of probability.

D. H. Mellor is Emeritus Professor of Philosophy at the University of Cambridge. His books include *The Facts of Causation* and *Real Time II*, both published by Routledge.

Probability:
A Philosophical Introduction

D. H. Mellor

Routledge
Taylor & Francis Group

LONDON AND NEW YORK

First published 2005
by Routledge
2 Park Square, Milton Park, Abingdon, Oxon OX14 4RN

Simultaneously published in the USA and Canada
by Routledge
270 Madison Ave, New York, NY 10016

Routledge is an imprint of the Taylor & Francis Group

Typeset in Palatino by the author
Printed and bound in Great Britain by
TJ International Ltd, Padstow, Cornwall

British Library Cataloguing in Publication Data
A catalogue record for this book is available from the British Library.

Library of Congress Cataloging in Publication Data
A catalog record for this book has been requested.

ISBN 0-415-28250-0 hbk
ISBN 0-415-28251-9 pbk

In memory of Frank Ramsey, Richard Braithwaite,
David Lewis and Dick Jeffrey

Contents

10 Chance, Frequency and Credence

Preface

This book derives from many years of introducing philosophy students to ideas of probability that impinge on other philosophical topics. That experience has convinced me that these ideas need to be in the intellectual tool-kit of all serious philosophers, just as the basic ideas of logic are. But while the latter need is widely recognised, the former is not, a fact which seems to be part cause and part effect of a paucity of books that introduce conceptually interesting aspects of probability in a simple and unbiased way. This book is partly an attempt to fill that gap. But only partly, since ideas from other areas of philosophy can shed as much light on probability as it does on them. So this book is meant not just for philosophers but for everyone who has occasion to use ideas of probability and is interested in their implications.

This book owes much to many people. First, to students who attended my courses on the subject, and from whose reactions I learned a great deal about what those courses should cover, and how. Second, to the many philosophers of probability from whose work I have learned what I know about the subject. Third, and most importantly, to Arnold Koslow, for much invaluable advice and help in structuring and preparing early drafts of this book.

Comments from other people who have read parts of drafts of the book have helped me to improve it. In particular, Hallvard Lillehammer's helped me to make early drafts less dense, and Peter Smith's to make the Introduction clearer. Alan Hájek and an anonymous referee read and commented in detail on the whole book in its penultimate form, and their reports both prompted and aided a very necessary final revision. I am especially grateful to Alan Hájek, whose exceptionally perceptive comments have saved me from several serious errors. Finally, I am greatly indebted to Craig Bourne for indexing the book and for compiling lists of further reading.

D. H. MELLOR
Cambridge
January 2005

Introduction and Summary

I

Introduction

The object of this book is to explain ideas of probability that philosophers and others may need or want to understand. While this means introducing some elementary mathematics of probability, very little mathematical expertise is required to follow it, and the book contains no exercises to test or increase that expertise. In this respect it differs from some other introductions to probability written by or for philosophers, and also from most introductions to logic. In other respects, however, the book does provide material for introductory courses in probability analogous to those in logic. The former are indeed less common, partly because the need for them, although in my view no less, is less widely felt, and partly because there are, for this reason, few suitable textbooks for them. This I hope will become one of them.

However, this book is not meant only as a textbook. We all invoke probability from time to time, in contexts ranging from gambling, the law, insurance and economics, to epidemiology, genetics and quantum physics. Anyone wishing to acquire a little more understanding of these and other applications of probability will, I trust, find what follows of some interest.

To see why this book does what it does, it may help to look further at the analogy with introductory logic courses. The reason philosophy students are taught logic is not that they are expected to become logicians: they are not. Nor is it just because they must learn how to dissect arguments to assess their validity, although of course they do. But that after all is an ability we all need to some degree, and if some philosophical arguments are unusually hard to dissect, that is still not the main reason for teaching philosophers logic.

The main reason is that many topics in philosophy cannot be mastered without first mastering some basic logical ideas. No one for example can master the idea of laws of nature without grasping the logic of generality. Nor can we see how to deny the existence of God without seeing how 'God exists' can make sense if there is no God for 'God' to refer to. And while mastering such ideas, of generality and existence, may involve acquiring some proficiency in symbolic logic, that is neither the main object of the exercise nor a substitute for it. Thus, to take another example, learning to apply a mechanical test for tautologousness in the propositional calculus is no substitute for learning what a tautology is and why it matters. That is something which anyone who wants to think straight needs to know, and is therefore something which all good courses in logic for non-logicians teach.

Similarly, if perhaps less obviously, with probability. If we all need some grasp of ideas and theories of logic to understand logical aspects of other topics, we also need some grasp of ideas and theories of probability, for a similar reason. Within philosophy, for example, some of those ideas and theories are central to theories of causation and laws of nature, especially when these are taken to be indeterministic. Others are central to theories of evidence, and others again to theories of action and decision-making under risk or uncertainty. Trying to tackle the issues these theories raise without understanding how they involve probability is as hopeless as trying to tackle issues of existence without understanding its logic. Yet many philosophers and others who have all the logical understanding they need for these purposes still lack a sufficient grasp of ideas and theories of probability. It is that lack which this book aims, among other things, to remedy, while using a minimum of mathematics to do so.

Just as this book does not aim to teach the mathematics of probability, so too it does not tackle the intellectual and social history of ideas, theories and applications of probability, fascinating as that is. The history of probability, like its mathematics, is well covered by other books, as indeed is the job of teaching its philosophy to those interested in probability for its own sake. What this book tries to do, which others do not, is to give those who may not care about probability as such, as much understanding of it as they need for philosophical and other purposes.

One symptom of the need for a book like this is the number of philosophers and others who fail to refer to probability when they need to or who, if they do refer to it, fail to say what kind of probability – physical, subjective or epistemic – they mean, as if it did not matter, which it almost always does. Nor do enough of those who do distinguish these kinds of probability pay sufficient attention to persisting controversies about how they should be understood and related to each other. That situation too I would like this book to help to remedy.

If for these reasons this book assumes less prior knowledge of and interest in probability itself than do some other introductions to it, it does appeal to some basic philosophical ideas that are well covered in other standard courses and well-known books. As a textbook, therefore, this book will be most useful for philosophy students after their first undergraduate year, since they can then see how probability bears on other philosophical issues which they will already have encountered.

Another reason for encouraging readers to acquire some knowledge of philosophical ideas is that these can shed as much light on probability as it can on them. Enlightenment here can and should run both ways, as each of the kinds of probability mentioned above show. For example, if epistemic probability is to measure how far evidence supports hypotheses, then any view of it must fit a general view of what evidence is and what it does. Thus, as we shall see, so-called 'externalist' and 'internalist' views of evidence will require very different readings of epistemic probability. Those readings can therefore hardly be assessed independently of arguments for and against these two views of what evidence is. But as I hope most readers will already have some ideas about the nature of evidence, rival views of it will only be sketched in enough detail to show what they imply about epistemic probability.

Similarly with subjective probabilities, here also called credences, understood as measures of how strongly we believe things. My credence in a proposition A is, for example, often defined by the odds I would choose for a hypothetical bet on A's truth if all influences on my choice, other than my credence in A, were removed. This assumes, among other things, that beliefs come by degrees, that they and their degrees are definable by the actions they would combine with various desires to cause, and that they are also introspectible, since these actions are mostly hypothetical. These assumptions about belief are far too contentious to be taken for granted, as they often are by theorists of probability. Drawing them out should therefore be as enlightening to probability theorists as their theories in turn should be to philosophers and others interested in how what we think affects how we act.

Similarly too with physical probabilities, here also called chances, like the chances of our catching infectious diseases, or winning lotteries, or of coin tosses landing heads. As we shall see, different theories of chance take chances to measure very different things. One takes them to measure physical possibilities, like the possibility of catching a disease when we are exposed to it. Another takes chances to measure hypothetical frequencies, such as how frequently you would win a lottery if you kept on buying tickets for it. While a third takes chances to measure dispositions, e.g. of a coin to land heads more or less often when repeatedly tossed in the same way. All these theories raise modal and meta-physical questions – about what possibilities and dispositions are, and what makes hypothetical or counterfactual statements true – which need to be taken into account in assessing the pros and cons of these theories of chance.

It is for these reasons that views and arguments in other parts of philosophy will be cited when they seem relevant, one way or the other, to the aspects of probability dealt with in this book. In deciding which views and arguments to bring in, and in how much detail, I have been guided by what I think most readers are likely to know about them. Some readers will therefore find that, for them, too much is said about some topics and too little about others. For this I can only apologise and hope that where too much is said readers will skip or skim and, where too little, that references given at the ends of chapters may help to amplify or clarify what is said.

II

Summary

The contents of the book are as follows. Chapter 1 starts by distinguishing and illustrating the three principal applications of numerical probability. These are to physical probabilities or chances; to degrees of belief or credences; and to epistemic probabilities. The idea of conditional probability is then introduced, a few basic rules of numerical probability are stated, and the distinction between pure and applied probability is drawn and clarified. Here, as throughout the book, the issues and arguments are presented using simple examples requiring only the most elementary mathematics. (In particular, applications of probability to infinities will only be discussed where it seems to me essential to do so.)

Chapter 2 introduces the classical conception of probability as a measure of possibility. It shows how two of our three kinds of probability, epistemic and physical, may be taken to measure corresponding kinds of possibility – epistemic and metaphysical – that are familiar to philosophers. The terminology of sample spaces is then presented in a simple case, to enable the classical principle of indifference to be illustrated and assessed, as applied first to epistemic probabilities and then to chances.

This leads in chapter 3 to an exposition and assessment of frequency theories of probability. Like the classical theory, these theories do not apply to credences; nor are they easily applied to the epistemic probabilities of singular propositions, such as the proposition that a particular smoker will get cancer. Frequency theories are really credible only as theories of chance, where they are shown to fit and extend a Humean 'constant conjunction' view of causation and of laws of nature. By comparing them with the classical view of chance we can also see how they extend the Humean substitute for natural necessity – invariable conjunction – into a substitute for the classical idea of quantitative natural possibility, namely more or less frequent conjunctions, such as the proportions of people exposed to an infectious disease who actually catch it. The chapter ends by showing how the problems of equating chances with actual frequencies lead naturally to the development first of limiting frequency, and then of hypothetical limiting frequency, theories of chance.

In chapter 4, two other theories of chance are explained and assessed. One is a modal theory which keeps the classical idea of chance as a measure of possibility while rejecting the classical thesis that numbers of 'ultimate equipossibilities' are what provide this measure. Instead, it takes physical possibilities to be measured by the hypothetical limiting frequencies they explain, a thesis illustrated by a simple application of the so-called 'ergodic hypothesis'. The modal theory is then contrasted with the propensity theory, which identifies so-called 'single-case' chances with dispositions to produce limiting frequencies; and the latter theory is then shown to differ from a hypothetical limiting frequency theory only on a realist view of dispositions. This is followed by a discussion of the crucial difference between the modal and propensity theories: the fact that, for any proposition A, the modal theory makes 'The chance that A is true is 1' entail A, whereas the propensity theory – like the limiting frequency theories – does not.

Chapter 5 turns from chance to credence, understood as a probability measure of degrees of belief. It starts by making the case for thinking that beliefs do come by degrees, after which it presents and discusses betting arguments for a probability measure of those degrees. Some unattractive implications of this, e.g. that we all believe every necessary truth, are used to introduce the debate about whether credences measure our actual degrees of belief, or those we would have if only we were rational. This leads, via the idea that credences lack precise values, to an elementary exposition of subjective decision theory, interpreted as a generalisation of how we do or should choose odds for bets.

The topic of chapter 6 is the confirmation of hypotheses, understood as the credence, if any, that we should have in hypotheses given our evidence about them – a reading which automatically gives confirmation a probability measure. It is not assumed that confirmation must be measured in this way, merely that doing so enables us to discuss in probabilistic terms many of the important philosophical questions posed by inconclusive evidence. Because the epistemic probabilities of hypotheses, unlike chances and credences, are relative to evidence, they are non-empirical, since new evidence generates a new relation rather than confirming or disconfirming an existing one.

This feature of epistemic probabilities raises the question of whether confirmation is a logical relation, like entailment, which would make confirmation theory an extension of the deductive logic of conclusive evidence to an inductive logic of inconclusive evidence. It is argued however that the real question is not whether confirmation relations are logical, but how we can discover their values. The difficulty of doing this *a priori* is taken to show that confirmation relations may be no more than idle intermediaries between our evidence about hypotheses and the credence it entitles us to have in them.

Chapter 7 takes us from general questions about the nature of confirmation to the specific and influential but still contentious Bayesian theory of conditionalisation. This equates the probability of a hypothesis A given evidence B with A's probability conditional on B, where this is equated with the probability of the conjunction of A and B prior to our learning that B is true, divided by the prior probability of B. After giving a standard sample space argument for this equation, problems posed by its reliance on prior probabilities are argued to be soluble only if these are interpreted as credences. Even then the problem remains of how to justify specific values of prior credences, and the chapter ends by introducing Bayes's Theorem as a possible solution to that problem.

Chapter 8 follows this up by asking what might justify not only our prior credences but also the 'input' credences that prompt conditionalisation, for example, an input credence 1 in B caused by seeing that B is true, as opposed to the 'output' credence in A that conditionalising on B then produces. After considering how perception might justify input credences, we turn to output credences, and look first at how so-called coherence theories of the justification of full beliefs can be applied to output credences that are less than 1. Then, after sketching some arguments for this idea of justification, we see how a rival reliabilist idea – that full beliefs are justified if they have a high chance of being true – can also be extended to apply to output credences that are less than 1. This in turn prompts an account of how conditionalisation itself can be generalised to deal with uncertain evidence, i.e. evidence which produces input credences that fall short of full belief.

The Bayesian way of updating credences in response to evidence having been outlined, chapter 9 raises various questions for it and looks at possible answers to them. First, we see why the generalised conditionalisation sketched at the end of chapter 8 cannot be justified by the sample space argument for basic conditionalisation given in chapter 7. Then a proposition in Bayes's original paper is shown to support conditionalisation psychologically, if not logically. The next question tackled is how to conditionalise when conditional credences are undefined, as they often are in decision-making, when we are trying to decide whether to make a proposition true or false. After that, the use of our choice of odds for conditional bets to justify conditionalisation is examined and argued to be inconclusive. Finally, the implications for Bayesianism are considered of the existence of rival rules for updating credences, and of empirical evidence that we often update our credences in very non-Bayesian ways.

The last chapter starts by outlining the link between chances and the actual frequencies which they are supposed to explain, and which provide our best estimates of those chances. The link, which I call the Large Numbers Link, is stated for a simple coin-tossing example, where what makes it hold is the probabilistic independence of the results of different tosses. This presents subjectivists with the problem of how to make the link hold without postulating the chances needed to define independence. Their concept of exchangeability, which solves that problem, is then explained, and applied to the coin-tossing case. Finally, the question is raised of how far this subjective surrogate for independence supports a subjectivist rejection of chances, and the answer is argued to be: not far enough. For while, for example, my credence 0.5 that a coin will land heads on any one of a hundred exchangeable tosses can explain why I am almost certain that the frequency of heads in those tosses will lie between 0.4 and 0.6, it cannot explain why that frequency does lie within that interval. The only kind of probability which can explain this fact, when it is a fact, is the coin's chance of landing heads.

Further Reading

The classic text on the probability calculus is Kolmogorov (1933). But much more accessible and useful for non-mathematicians, with a simple and impartial exposition of the calculus, are Kyburg (1970), part I, chapter 2, and Howson and Urbach (1993), chapter 2. For a survey of different interpretations of probability, see Humphreys (1998). A short general overview of the history of probability from about 1650 to about 1800 is given in chapter 1 of Gillies (2000). Hacking gives a more detailed history, from the fifteenth to the eighteenth centuries in his (1975), and in the nineteenth century in his (1990). Gigerenzer et al. (1989) provides an excellent survey of the impact of probability on science and everyday life from the seventeenth to the twentieth centuries. A mathematically more demanding account of the development of probability theory in the last century, with its applications in modern physics, is given in von Plato (1994).

1
Kinds of Probability

I

Introduction

We all use probability and related ideas all the time. To explain and relate all these applications we shall need to regiment our presentation of them in one or two ways. One is by ignoring trivial verbal variations, such as the use of 'likely' for 'probable'. Another and more important way is by classifying probabilities into three basic kinds: *physical*, *epistemic* and *subjective*. Physical probabilities will, for brevity, also be called *chances* and subjective probabilities *credences*.

Here are two examples of each kind of probability.

Chances:

Smokers have a greater chance of getting cancer than non-smokers have.

This coin toss is unbiased: it has equal chances of landing heads and tails.

Epistemic probabilities:

Astronomical data makes it very probable that our universe had a beginning.

New evidence makes it unlikely (= improbable) that the butler did it.

Credences:

I think it will probably rain tonight.

I'll bet you 4:1 that Pink Gin doesn't win the Derby.

The basis of this classification seems to be something like the following.

Chances are real features of the world. They show up, in these examples, in how often people get cancer and coin tosses land heads, and they are affected by whether people smoke, and by how coins are tossed. Chances are what they are whether or not we ever conceive of or know about them, and so they are neither relative to evidence nor mere matters of opinion, with no opinion any better than any other.

Epistemic probabilities seem not to be real features of the world in this sense. They only measure how far evidence confirms or disconfirms hypotheses about the world, for example that our world had a beginning or that the butler did it. But they are not mere matters of opinion: whether, and to what extent, evidence counts for or against a hypothesis looks like an objective matter.

Credences measure how strongly we believe propositions, like the proposition that it will rain tonight, or that Pink Gin will win the Derby. They are features of the people whose credences they are rather than features of what the credences are about. My low credence in Pink Gin's winning the Derby is more a fact about me than it is about Pink Gin or the Derby. By this I mean that my low credence that Pink Gin will win is a mere matter of my opinion, which need not be justified by any corresponding physical or epistemic probability. In particular, there is no contradiction in your credence in Pink Gin winning being higher than mine even if we both know all there is to know about the race: that after all is why you take my bet.

There is a third way in which our discussion of probabilities will need to be regimented: in terminology. As well as replacing 'likely' and 'unsure' with explicitly probabilistic terms, we shall need a general term for whatever may be called more or less probable, as in 'It will probably rain tonight'. What is said to be probable here may be called an *event*, a *fact* or a *state of affairs*, but for our purposes *proposition* will be better, as in 'the proposition that it will rain tonight'. The point is that there can be a probability of rain tonight even if it does not rain tonight, in which case that event, fact or state of affairs will not exist. But the proposition will: it will just not be true. (In what follows it will not matter what propositions are, nor how their truth is related to that of sentences or statements, issues which we therefore need not discuss.)

So by the probability of any proposition A, written 'P(A)', I shall mean the probability that A is true, for example that it really will rain tonight. The three kinds of probability I shall distinguish where necessary by writing 'CH(...)' for chances, 'EP(...)' for epistemic probabilities and 'CR(...)' for credences. Where I write 'P(...)' I mean what I say to apply to all probabilities.

Despite the initial plausibility of this division of probabilities, it remains to be seen how different our three kinds really are. A's chance might for example just be A's epistemic probability relative to all the relevant evidence we have or could get. A's epistemic probability might in turn just be the credence in A that we ought to have given our evidence about it. And my credence in A might just be what I think A's chance or epistemic probability is. These however are contentious claims, which we shall discuss in more detail later, where we could not even state them without drawing a provisional distinction between these kinds of probability.

Pending our later discussion, we must not read too much into the above labels for kinds of probability, and the cursory explanations of them. It is not easy to say, for example, what kind of entities chances are: different theories tell different stories, as we shall see, and some theories deny that any such entities exist at all. Similarly with credences, whose existence is also disputed, since some philosophers deny that belief comes by the degrees that credences are supposed to measure. Similarly with epistemic probabilities, which are no less contentious. Some philosophers deny, for example, that evidence which fails to falsify a scientific theory confirms it to any positive degree; while others, who admit that such confirmation is possible, decline to use probabilities to measure it.

These are among the controversies that call for caution in reading our labels, which are not meant to define the probabilities they stand for, still less to show that such probabilities exist. Their purpose is simply to draw some provisional distinctions without begging too many of the questions we shall discuss later.

Meanwhile the best way to show what the labels are meant to stand for is to give some more, and more serious, examples.

II

Chances

The role of chance in modern physics is hard to overstate. Theories of microphysics now ascribe chances to (propositions about) almost all small-scale events. These include the interactions of subatomic particles, and the transformations of atoms on which both nuclear power and nuclear weapons depend. How similar all these physical applications of numerical probability are is indeed a moot point, although most philosophers of physics would agree that they all fit the minimal assumptions I have made about chances, which are all we need to distinguish chances from credences and epistemic probabilities.

This is why, to avoid raising controversial but irrelevant questions about, e.g. the role of probability in quantum theory, I shall stick to its simplest and least contentious microphysical application, to radioactivity. On the well-established theory of this, all unexcited atoms of a given radioelement have an equal chance of decaying in any given interval of time. Atoms of radium, for instance, have a 50/50 chance of decaying within a definite period, of about 1600 years, which is, for that reason, called its *half life*.

My calling chances *physical* probabilities must not however be taken to imply that they figure only in physics. On the contrary, they figure in almost all modern sciences. There are the chances of the mutations on whose natural selection the generation and evolution of plant and animal species depends. Then there are the chances needed by natural selection itself: the chances of individuals with various genetic traits surviving to produce offspring with those traits.

Chances are also essential to explanations of how epidemics of infectious diseases like influenza start, spread and die away. What explains the course and duration of these epidemics is the way the chances of infection rise with the proportion of those already infected, and are reduced by vaccination and by immunity produced by the disease itself.

Psychology too involves chances, some of them with obvious practical implications. Take the way our chances of misremembering arbitrary numbers rise with the number of digits in them. Our chances of remembering four digit numbers correctly are high, which is why PINs have only four digits. Thereafter our chances of misremembering numbers rise rapidly, which is one reason why credit card numbers are so long.

This example, like that of epidemics, shows how chances can be as important in practice as they are in theory. Reducing the chances of illness, and raising those of recovery from it, are the core concerns of medicine and public health. Making road, rail and air travel safer is a matter of reducing the chance of death and injury it involves. Insurance premiums are based on assessments of the chances of whatever is insured against. And so on and so on.

Chances, in short, are everywhere, and not only in the games of chance to which much of the modern theory of probability was originally applied. It may therefore seem surprising that anyone should deny, as many philosophers have done, that there is in reality any such thing as chance. That denial will become less surprising when we see how hard it is to say what chance is, and how many rival theories of it there are. That however is the business of later chapters. Here I aim only to show the apparent ubiquity of chance, which is what makes understanding it so important.

III

Epistemic Probabilities

If the probabilities postulated by scientific theories are chances, those used to assess these and other theories are epistemic. Take one of the examples given in section I, only put the other way round: the low probability that our universe has existed for ever as opposed to having a beginning. That probability is not a chance, in the sense of being a feature of the world, like the chances of radium atoms decaying within intervals of future time. If the universe did have a beginning, there was never a time when it had some chance, however small, of not having one. The probabilities of these rival 'big bang' and 'steady state' theories are not physical but epistemic. That is to say, they measure the extent to which the astronomical and other physical evidence now available confirms the big bang theory as opposed to its steady state rival.

Epistemic probabilities are not confined to physics, any more than chances are. All scientists need evidence in order to decide between rival hypotheses, including hypotheses about the values of chances, whose truth may matter in practice as well as in theory. Take the question of whether to be vaccinated in an epidemic of flu. To make that decision we need some idea of our chances of catching flu if we are vaccinated and if we are not. But these chances, like most chances, are not directly observable. (This is one reason for questioning their existence.) So to estimate them we need evidence that *is* observable, such as the proportions of vaccinated and of unvaccinated people who catch flu when exposed to it. And then – setting aside the philosophical problem of induction – we need to know how far this statistical evidence supports alternative hypotheses about the values of these chances. The principles which statisticians use to answer such questions are themselves contentious, as we shall see, and not all of them give the answers as probabilities. But if they do, then a probability of say 0.95 that my chance of catching flu will be 0.3±0.1 if I am vaccinated and 0.6±0.1 if I am not, is epistemic rather than physical.

As in medicine, so in the law. In civil courts, where plaintiffs are required to establish their case 'on the balance of probabilities', these probabilities are also epistemic. Similarly in criminal courts, where the prosecution has to show that the defendant is guilty 'beyond reasonable doubt'. The much higher probability of guilt needed to meet this criterion is again epistemic, as we can see in another of the examples given in section I: the probability, in a classic English country house murder mystery, that the butler did it.

For in this case it is not sufficient for the defence to show that the *chance* of the butler being the murderer was low, as indeed it might have been. (Suppose for example he was chosen at random from hundreds of would-be assassins.) That is irrelevant: what matters is the probability relative to the evidence before the court that the butler *was* the murderer. It is that epistemic probability which the prosecution needs to show is high enough to justify a guilty verdict and the defence needs to show is not so.

Similarly in less melodramatic examples. Suppose you see a tossed coin land on edge. Suppose moreover that you are awake, sober and have good eyesight, that the scene is well lit and there are no conjurors around. In these conditions, the coin's very low *chance* of landing on edge does little or nothing to reduce the very high epistemic probability that it did so, relative to the evidence of your senses. Here too there seems a clear distinction between the chance and the epistemic probability of a proposition's being true. And this is true, even if we say, as some do, that once a coin has landed heads, it has a high *chance* of having done so, namely 1: for this is still not the same as the epistemic probability that it landed heads, which need not be *that* high.

The same distinction applies, as we have already noted, to doctors testing vaccines and other treatments in order to decide whether or not to use them. In testing treatments, as opposed to prescribing them, it is epistemic probabilities, not chances, that matter. Similarly in testing any scientific theory to see whether the results of the tests confirm the theory strongly enough to justify accepting it, i.e. using it to predict and explain observable phenomena. If the support which such empirical evidence gives a theory is measured by a probability, that probability will be epistemic rather than physical.

Epistemic probabilities seem therefore to be just as ubiquitous and as important as chances. For besides their role in philosophical theories of what knowledge is, our examples show how they are needed to explain how court-room and other testimony works, and the nature of scientific method generally, and especially of statistical testing.

IV

Credences

In section I two examples were given of statements that seem to express credences, understood as degrees of belief:

'I think it will probably rain tonight.' and
'I'll bet you 4:1 that Pink Gin doesn't win the Derby.'

It is however debatable whether these or any other statements really express any such thing. It might be that what they express is never a *degree* of belief, high or low, in a proposition A, e.g. that Pink Gin will win the Derby, but rather the so-called *full* belief that A has a high or low chance or epistemic probability of being true. If that is so, and belief itself does not come by degrees, then the probability which I take a proposition to have will no more be a psychological kind of probability than my thinking it's hot outside is a psychological kind of temperature.

Against this on-off view of belief must be set the evident possibility of *doubting* A, a state of mind lying between full belief in A and full disbelief in it and coming by degrees that seem to reflect degrees of belief in A. Then there are so-called decision theories, which exploit the idea that, by and large, we do what we most strongly believe will get us what we want. These theories credit us with credences – degrees of belief – and subjective utilities – degrees of desire – which determine how we will or should act: saying for example that people will not or should not bet at 4:1 that Pink Gin will win unless their credences that he will are at least $1/(1+4)$. It is not easy to make sense of this and much other, even more important, prudential advice unless belief comes by degrees.

And given this positive case for degrees of belief, we have other reasons for not identifying them with full beliefs in corresponding chances or epistemic probabilities. Suppose, for example, I am about to toss a coin that is either two-tailed or two-headed, and you don't know which, so your *credence* in its landing heads is $1/2$. Yet you certainly do not believe that the coin's *chance* of landing heads is $1/2$: on the contrary, you know it is either 0 or 1. Nor need you believe that the *epistemic* probability of heads is $1/2$, since you may know that you have *no* evidence about which kind of coin I am about to toss and – for reasons to be given in chapter 2.VI – you do not think that this ignorance makes the epistemic probability of heads $1/2$. That need not stop your credence in heads being $1/2$ for what even you recognise is no good reason.

V

How Kinds of Probability Differ

We have already seen several apparent differences between our three kinds of probability. Chances differ from credences in being features of the world, as opposed to features of our beliefs about the world. And while, as we shall see, some theories make chances relative to classifications of things – e.g. giving me different chances of getting a heart attack depending on whether I am classified by my age, by my diet or by how much I smoke – neither chances nor credences are relative to *evidence*. My chance of getting a heart attack may depend on whether I am classified by my age or by my diet; it does not depend on what evidence there is about how old I am or about what I eat.

Epistemic probabilities, on the other hand, unlike chances and credences, *are* relative to evidence. A contingent proposition may therefore have different epistemic probabilities relative to different possible pieces of evidence. Thus the epistemic probability that Pink Gin will win the Derby may be much greater relative to evidence of the horse's past triumphs than to evidence of his recent lameness. How these different probabilities are to be taken account of in deciding at what odds to bet that the horse will win this race is, as we shall see, a hard question. But before we can tackle it we must first ask what epistemic probabilities are and, in particular, what fixes their values.

One theory is that the values of epistemic probabilities are fixed by a kind of logic, a so-called *inductive logic*, conceived as a generalisation of deductive logic. For if B entails A, so that A cannot be false if B is true, then relative to B the epistemic probability of A's negation (which I shall write '¬A') must be 0, and that of A must be 1. Weaker logical relations between A and other propositions may then be postulated to correspond to other values of epistemic probability. This, however, is a contentious view of what epistemic probabilities measure, as we shall see in chapter 6. And even if it is right, the values of these intermediate probabilities are certainly far harder to derive from any logic than chances are from physical theories, or than our credences are from our decisions about (for example) what odds to back horses at. For the time being, the source of epistemic probabilities must remain an open question.

VI

Probabilities of Complex Propositions

Is the chance of throwing at least one 6 in four throws of a single die greater than that of throwing at least one double 6 in twenty-four throws of two dice? This question, posed by the Chevalier de Méré in the seventeenth century, is typical of the gaming examples that prompted the modern development of probability theory. It looks like a question about how to discover the chances of certain contingent propositions, e.g. that at least one of four throws of a die will be a 6. But the question is really about how to derive some such chances from others, because it assumes that the chance of getting a 6 on any one throw of a single die is 1/6. How we know that is another matter, de Méré's question being what this knowledge tells us about the chances of more complex propositions.

Questions like de Méré's do not only arise for gamblers, as the following example shows. In most populations, slightly more boys are born than girls, roughly in the ratio 18:17. Suppose this statistic reflects a corresponding chance, of just over 1/2, that a birth will be of a boy. Then the chance that, out of 14,000 infants, between 7037 and 7363 will be boys, is 43 to 1, i.e. nearly 0.98.

Now it may not be obvious how so detailed an estimate of the number of males in a large group of infants can be inferred from the comparative chances of male and female births. If the inference is correct, it suggests that the probabilities involved are indeed chances, i.e. features of the world, as we have been assuming. But this does not really follow. For the inference is not that between 7037 and 7363 out of 14,000 infants *will* be male, a conclusion about the world that is indeed direct and easily checked, but merely that the probability that this is so is very high.

In short, the inference here, as in the gambling case, is really only from one probability to another. So in both cases it is premature to conclude that all the probabilities are chances. The most we can say so far is that they are all of the same kind, whether that be physical, epistemic or personal. And whichever they are, the same questions arise, which we shall discuss later: what fixes the values of these probabilities; and what makes one such probability follow from another?

VII

Conditional Probabilities

Suppose the probability of a coin toss landing heads is $1/2$, and compare these two questions.

(a) What is the probability that two such tosses will both land heads?
(b) What is the probability of the second toss landing heads, given that the first toss lands heads?

Question (a) is another question of the kind we have just looked at, namely how to derive one probability from others. In this case the probability to be derived is that of a conjunction, $A \wedge B$, of the propositions A, that the second toss lands heads, and B, that the first one does. This probability, $P(A \wedge B)$, is easily derived if the tosses are *independent* in a sense to be further discussed in chapter 10.III, for then $P(A \wedge B)$ is equal to the product of the probabilities of its conjuncts A and B, so that

(1.1) $P(A \wedge B) = P(A) \times P(B) = 1/2 \times 1/2 = 1/4.$

The probability in (b), on the other hand, is A's probability *conditional* on B, meaning the probability that A is true given that B is true. This is standardly written '$P(A \mid B)$' and standardly assumed, if $P(B) > 0$, to satisfy the equation

(1.2) $P(A \mid B) = \dfrac{P(A \wedge B)}{P(B)}.$

Here the idea is that A will be independent of B – meaning that B tells us nothing about A's prospects of being true – if $P(A \mid B)$ is equal to A's *unconditional* probability $P(A)$, thus making

(1.3) $P(A \mid B) = P(A) = 1/2.$

This distinction between conditional and unconditional probabilities is important in all three kinds of probability. Its significance, however, differs in each case, and is not always clear, as we can see in our coin-tossing example by looking at the different ways in which the two tosses may be said to be independent.

First, if the probabilities of the tosses landing heads are physical, the basic probability is the *unconditional* physical probability – the chance – $1/2$ of heads on each toss. On some theories this chance may indeed, as we noted in section V, be relative to how the toss is classified, e.g. by a more or less detailed description of how the coin is tossed. But given that classification, the chance of this toss landing heads is an unconditional physical fact about the world, and one which fixes all the other unconditional and conditional probabilities of similarly classified tosses landing heads in a way which is yet to be explained but which we may assume is also physical. So in particular, what makes the unconditional and the conditional chances of heads on the second toss equal is also a physical fact, namely that the result of the first toss does not physically affect the chance of heads on the second toss: the tosses are *physically* independent.

If the probabilities in this example are credences, the basic one will again be unconditional: my credence $CR(A) = 1/2$ in each toss landing heads. But then this credence must fix my other credences in a *psychological* rather than a physical way. If my conditional and unconditional credences in heads on the second toss are equal – i.e. if $CR(A|B) = CR(A)$ – this will not be because A is physically independent of B, but because it is psychologically independent: I think that learning that the first toss landed heads will not affect my credence in the second toss landing heads.

Epistemic probabilities are different again. Here, because these probabilities are explicitly relative to evidence, the basic concept is that of *conditional* probability. On this reading, therefore, the apparently unconditional probability $P(A)$, that the second toss lands heads, is really the probability, $EP(A|K)$, of A conditional on some background evidence K, e.g. about how the coin is tossed. Then, when we acquire our new evidence B, that the first toss lands heads, this is added to K to yield the conjunction $K \wedge B$. So we say then that, given K, heads on the second toss will be *epistemically* independent of heads if A's probability given $K \wedge B$ is equal to its probability given K, i.e. if

$$EP(A|K \wedge B) = EP(A|K) = 1/2.$$

Similarly for all A, B and K: if $EP(A|K \wedge B) = EP(A|K)$ then, relative to K, A is epistemically independent of B, and B is therefore evidentially irrelevant to A, being evidence neither for A nor against it.

VIII

Numerical Probabilities

In all our examples I have called propositions not just probable or improbable, but also more or less probable, implying thereby that probability comes by degrees. This does not, however, entail that all probabilities have numerical values, since they might be comparative without being quantitative. That is, they might be greater or less than each other without anything fixing by *how much* they are greater or less. Still, important links hold even among merely comparative probabilities. To express these, let A be any more or less probable proposition (say that it will rain tonight) and ¬A its negation. Then

> A is *probable* only if
>> A is *more probable than not*, i.e. only if
>> A is *more probable* than ¬A

(it being a tricky but trivial question *how much* more probable A must be than ¬A before we will call it probable).

This link between being probable and being more probable that not holds on any reading of 'A is probable', provided that 'A is more probable than not' and 'A is more probable than ¬A' are read in the same way: i.e. as chances (relative if need be to the same classification), or as epistemic probabilities relative to the same evidence, or as the credences of one person at a single time.

If A does have a numerical probability, $P(A)$, the following rules also apply:

> (1.4) All probabilities lie between 0 and 1 inclusive, i.e.
>> $0 \le P(A) \le 1$.
>
> (1.5) The probabilities of A and of ¬A always add up to 1, i.e.
>> $P(A) + P(\neg A) = 1$; so that
>
> (1.6) A is probable and ¬A improbable only if
>> $P(A) > 1/2 > P(\neg A)$.

Note that rules like these, whose rationales we shall discuss later, do not fix the probability of any one contingent proposition, such as the proposition that it will rain tonight. That probability, if there is one, is fixed by meteorological facts if it is physical, by meteorological evidence if it is epistemic and by our credences in rain if it is subjective. All the rules do is show how the probability of one such proposition A affects those of logically related ones, such as A's negation, ¬A.

Other rules will be given later; but some should be given now, as some of them have been used already. For example, I said in section V that the epistemic probability of a proposition conditional on evidence which entails it is 1; and this rule applies to all numerical probabilities, not just epistemic ones. In symbols, if '⇒' means 'entails', then for all propositions A and B,

> (1.7) If $A \Rightarrow B$, then if $P(B) = 1$, $P(A) = 1$.

This follows from the more basic rule that

> (1.8) No proposition is more probable than any proposition it entails, i.e.
>> If $A \Rightarrow B$, then $P(A) \le P(B)$.

(It cannot, for example, be more probable that Pink Gin will win the Derby by finishing *first* than that Pink Gin will at least *finish*.) From (1.8) it follows that all logically equivalent propositions have the same probability, i.e. that

> (1.9) If $A \Leftrightarrow B$, then $P(A) = P(B)$.

Another important rule of numerical probability is that

(1.10) All necessary propositions have probability 1; and
(1.11) All impossible propositions have probability 0.

And because, by definition, necessary propositions cannot be false, in particular they cannot be false if any other proposition is true. Similarly, because impossible propositions cannot be true, they cannot be true if any other proposition is false. From this, given that, by definition of entailment, for any propositions A and B,

$$A \Rightarrow B \text{ if and only if it is impossible for A to be true and B false,}$$

it follows that

> every proposition entails all *necessary* propositions, and
> every proposition is entailed by all *impossible* propositions.

This and (1.8) entail that no proposition's probability can be greater than that of a necessary proposition or less than that of an impossible one: hence the rule (1.4), that all probabilities lie between 0 and 1 inclusive.

Another rule that should be stated now, often called the *additivity principle*, may be thought of as a generalisation of (1.5). It says that for any propositions A and B whose conjunction $A \wedge B$ is impossible, the probability of their disjunction, written '$A \vee B$', is given by

(1.12) If $A \wedge B$ is impossible, $P(A \vee B) = P(A) + P(B)$.

All these rules hold for *all* kinds of probabilities, given the provisos stated above, e.g. that if they are credences, they are credences of the same person at the same time. Similarly, on an epistemic reading, all the apparently unconditional probabilities in these rules, like $P(A)$, must be read as probabilities, like $P(A \mid K)$, conditional on the same background evidence K.

It is not, however, obvious that even these provisos suffice to make all *credences* satisfy our rules, for it is not obvious that they suffice to make credences satisfy (1.8). For suppose that, although A entails B, I do not realise that it does: can I not think A more probable than B, i.e. have a greater credence in A?

I say not: because, as we shall see in chapter 5, (1.8) follows from assumptions that are needed to credit people with credences in the first place, so that not even for credences are (1.8)–(1.11) the optional extras they seem to be. Meanwhile, we may at least take (1.8) to say, of any credences $CR(A)$ and $CR(B)$ that any person x has at any given time t, that $CR(A) \le CR(B)$ if x fully believes at t that A entails B; and similarly for (1.9)–(1.11).

Finally, two other groups of rules, which follow from the above and other simple rules, should be put on record at this point. The first group concerns propositions with probability 1, and conjunctions with them, where the conjunction of A and B is, as before, written '$A \wedge B$'.

(1.13) If $P(A)$ is 1, then $P(\neg A)$ is 0.
(1.14) $P(A \wedge B)$ is 1 iff $P(A)$ and $P(B)$ are both 1.
(1.15) If $P(A)$ is 1, then for any B, $P(A \wedge B) = P(B)$.
(1.16) If $A \Rightarrow B$ and $P(A)$ is 1, then $P(B)$ is 1.

The second group concern propositions with probability 0, and disjunctions with them, where the disjunction of A with B, A or B, is, as before, written 'A∨B'.

(1.17) If P(A) is 0, then P(¬A) is 1.
(1.18) P(A∨B) is 0 iff P(A) and P(B) are both 0.
(1.19) If P(A) is 0, then for any B, P(A∨B) = P(B).
(1.20) If A ⇒ B and P(B) is 0, then P(A) is 0.

Both groups of rules may have a familiar ring to logicians, since they continue to hold if we replace 'P(A) is 1' with 'A is true' and 'P(A) is 0' with 'A is false': a fact which, as we shall see in chapter 8.II, has a bearing on the so-called coherence theory of truth.

IX

Pure and Applied Probability

The rules given in section VIII illustrate the fact that underlying all our three kinds of probability is another kind: numerical probability, defined not by the applications of probability but by the rules which, however probability is applied, govern its numerical values. These rules have been developed into a serious branch of mathematics, of which in this book we shall need only a very small and simple fragment. But the existence of mathematical probability does raise a terminological point which does need to be made here.

The point may be illustrated by a problem called Buffon's Needle problem. It is an example of so-called *geometric* probability, one of several that influenced modern probability theory, and especially the idea that probability is a *measure*, applied in this case to a geometrical space. The problem is this. Imagine a flat surface inscribed with parallel lines *n* units apart, on to which a needle of length *m* (less than *n*) is thrown at random, as shown in Figure 1. What is the probability that the needle will, after it lands, lie across one of the lines?

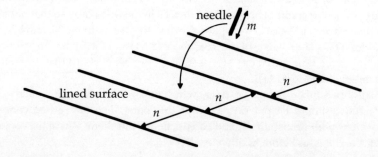

Figure 1: Buffon's Needle

The answer to this question – $2m/\pi n$ – is derived by taking 'at random' to mean here that the needle is equally likely to fall at any angle to the lines and with its centre in any equal area of the surface. Here therefore, as in section VI, the mathematics of probability is being used to infer one probability from others. Only in this case the initial probabilities, unlike those of births being male, or of dice landing 6, are not real chances, since they are fixed not by empirical facts but by mathematical assumption. That is what makes the problem purely mathematical, like calculating the sum (180°) of the angles of a Euclidean triangle.

But now suppose we have an actual device for throwing actual needles on to an actual lined surface, and want to know the needles' probabilities of landing across those actual lines. Now the question is no longer purely mathematical, since n, m, and the needles' probabilities of landing at various angles and places are facts about actual throws of actual needles. The probabilities here are real chances: no longer merely mathematical, but physical, like the sums of the angles of actual triangles on the earth's surface.

In short, just as we distinguish the pure geometry of Euclidean triangles from the applied geometry of terrestrial ones, so we need to distinguish purely mathematical probabilities from applied ones, whether these be physical (as in this case), epistemic or subjective. This is why mathematical probability is not really a fourth kind on a par with the other three but rather, as I remarked at the start of this section, a kind that underlies all the others.

The pure/applied distinction therefore applies to probability just as it does to geometry. But there is an important terminological difference. Euclid's is not the only mathematical system that is called a 'geometry', and in some of the others the angles of triangles add up to more than 180°. And so do those of real triangles on the earth's surface, like those bounded by the equator and two lines of longitude running from it to the north pole. In other words, the mathematics of large figures on the curved two-dimensional surface of the earth is not Euclidean. Yet we still describe this non-Euclidean mathematics as a '*geo*-metry', precisely because we use it (among other things) to measure such earthly figures. In short, it is not the mathematics of pure geometries that makes them *geometries* but one of their intended applications.

Here lies the difference. Usually, only measures that satisfy the rules given in section VIII are called 'probabilities'. That is because these rules fit natural measures of many obvious applications of probability, just as Euclid's axioms fit many obvious applications of geometry. But in some applications the standard rules of probability are less evidently right. This is especially so of theories of evidence, which may use quite different measures of how much propositions support each other. These so-called *non-probabilistic* theories of evidence may then fail to be compared to their probabilistic rivals, simply because they are not applications of the usual rules of numerical probability.

This seems to me wrong, because it puts form before content. Proper accounts of evidence should treat probabilistic and other theories of it on a par, just as accounts of geometry treat Euclidean and non-Euclidean geometries on a par. That, however, is beyond the scope of this book, and not just because it is an introduction to *probability*. The real reason is that presenting non-probabilistic theories of evidence would involve too much technicality, given that the questions about evidence that we need to discuss show up equally well in probabilistic theories of it; and similarly for chances and credences. This is why the only mathematics in this book is that of probability, and then only the minimum needed to discuss its important applications. For it is these applications, not their mathematics, which provide the material that justifies both the form and the content of this book.

Further Reading

In the so-called 'two-concept' view of probability advocated by Carnap in his (1945), reprinted in Feigl and Sellars (1949), and his (1955), what are here called physical and epistemic probabilities are called 'statistical' and 'inductive' and given frequency and logical interpretations (see chapters 3 and 5 below). The distinction between physical and subjective probabilities is drawn in Ramsey (1926), and the two are linked in Lewis (1980a) in a way that is closely related to the 'chances-as-evidence principle' of chapter 6 below. Chapter 8 of Gillies (2000) argues for a spectrum of kinds of probability between the subjective and the fully objective, and in particular for an 'intersubjective' kind of probability. Hájek (2001) surveys, among other things, non-standard theories of probability, discusses Carnap's view of logical probability, and gives many more references.

2
Classical Probabilities

I

Introduction

In chapter 1 probabilities were classified into three kinds: chances, epistemic probabilities and credences, satisfying the same mathematical rules. But this is not all that these kinds of probability have in common, as we can see by comparing them with three different kinds of waves: water, sound and light waves. These too share some mathematics, since they all have speeds V, frequencies F and wavelengths W, which in consistent units (such as metres per second, cycles per second and metres) satisfy the equation

$$V = F \times W.$$

They also have analogous empirical features, since they can all, for example, be reflected and refracted. But this is all they have in common. In particular, no facts about any of them imply anything about the others in the way that, as we saw in chapter 1.II, facts about chances, epistemic probabilities and credences do. For example, suppose we know, never mind how, that a coin toss has a chance p of landing heads. Relative to that evidence, the epistemic probability of the proposition A that the toss *will* land heads must also be p, which in turn makes p the credence that, in these circumstances, we should have in A. Links like these show that, unlike our three kinds of waves, our three kinds of probability must share more than their mathematics. They must either share an *interpretation* of that mathematics or, if they require different interpretations, those interpretations must between them explain why probabilities of these different kinds are linked as they are.

However, the mathematics of probability can be, and has been, interpreted in several different ways. In the next few chapters I shall introduce and illustrate these interpretations and see what sense each of them makes of our three kinds of probability. I start with the earliest, the therefore so-called *classical* interpretation, or *classicism* for short, most famously expounded by Laplace in the early nineteenth century. Here, however, we shall not follow Laplace's theory in detail, but only in some of its ideas, notably its basic idea that what probabilities measure are *possibilities*.

II

Two Kinds of Possibility

The idea that probabilities measure possibilities offers an interpretation of two of our three kinds of probability: chance and epistemic probability. To see how, we must first distinguish two different readings of the claim that a contingent proposition A, say that a coin toss lands heads, may or may not be true. One is that A might or might not be true, depending in our example on whether or not the toss lands heads. This kind of possibility I shall call *metaphysical* and take to be measured by A's *chance* of being true. The other reading of the claim that A may or may not be true is, in our example, that because we do not know how the coin toss lands, we do not *know* whether A is true. It is this *epistemic* kind of possibility that A's *epistemic probability*, given whatever we *do* know, measures.

This distinction, between metaphysical and epistemic possibilities, will be familiar to philosophers from other contexts. Take the two kinds of conditional statements often illustrated by the following instances, based on the assassination of US President John F. Kennedy by one Lee Harvey Oswald:

(2.1) 'If Oswald *did not* kill Kennedy, someone else *did*';
(2.2) 'If Oswald *had not* killed Kennedy, someone else *would have*'.

That (2.1) and (2.2) differ is shown by the fact that whereas (2.1) must be true, given that Kennedy was in fact killed, (2.2) may be false, since Oswald may have had no backup. One common explanation of this difference is that (2.1) is about our actual world, where someone, who may or may not have been Oswald, did kill Kennedy; whereas (2.2) is about a possible world, which may or may not be actual, where by definition Oswald did *not* kill Kennedy. (On the theory of Lewis (1973b), this is the possible world or worlds most like ours where Oswald did not kill Kennedy.)

This explanation of why (2.1) and (2.2) differ exploits the same distinction between epistemic and metaphysical possibilities that has just been introduced. To see this, let A be the proposition that Oswald did not kill Kennedy. Then the possibility that A is true hypothesised in (2.1) is the *epistemic* possibility that, in the actual world, Oswald did not kill Kennedy. Being epistemic, it is conditional on relevant evidence, which might for example show that no one else at the time was in a position to kill Kennedy in the way that he was killed. If our evidence, B, did show this, it would thereby show that Oswald *must* have killed Kennedy, but only in an epistemic sense of 'must', not in the sense that he was *compelled* to kill him. This then is the epistemic sense in which B leaves A *no* possibility of being true. It is also the sense in which, if different evidence B' showed that others *were* in a position to kill Kennedy at the time, B' *would* leave A possible. And if that possibility can come by degrees with a probability measure, then its probability will be as epistemic as the examples in chapter 1.III.

In (2.2), by contrast, the hypothesised possibility of A's truth is *metaphysical*. It is independent of evidence: for even the evidence B that leaves A no epistemic

possibility of truth will not show that, in a metaphysical sense, Oswald *had* to kill
Kennedy. However certain it is that he did, it can still have been metaphysically
possible that he would not, just as it can be metaphysically possible for a coin toss
to land heads even if it actually lands tails. And if this metaphysical possibility of
A's truth comes by degrees, with a probability measure, its probability will be no
less physical, i.e. no less a chance, than the examples in chapter 1.II.

III

Credences

Although the classical idea that probabilities measure possibilities applies
naturally to chances and epistemic probabilities, it does not apply at all to
credences. To see why not, suppose that a coin toss is fair and known to be fair.
That is, its chance of landing heads is known to be 1/2 and, relative to this
evidence, B, the epistemic probability of the proposition A, that the toss will in
fact land heads, is also 1/2. So if B is all I know about the coin toss, and if my
belief in A comes by probabilistic degrees, then its degree – my credence in A –
should also be 1/2.

This link between credence and epistemic probability does not however show
that credence also has a classical interpretation. All it shows is that my credence
in A should have the same value as the epistemic probability which I know A
has. But this does not tell us what credences are. Even if my belief in A's chance
or epistemic probability is a belief in a metaphysical or epistemic possibility,
having that belief is not the same thing as having a degree of belief in A itself. If it
were, then as we noted in chapter 1.IV, there would be no such thing as what I am
calling credence, and therefore no need to interpret it.

There is only one sense in which credences measure possibilities. This is the
sense in which the numerical value, 1/2, of my credence in A is a measure of a
possible credence, namely a credence in A which it is possible, metaphysically or
epistemically, for people to have. But that sense is irrelevant here, as we can see
by realising that numerical values of *all* quantities measure possibilities: as for
instance 100 on the Celsius scale, and 212 on the Fahrenheit scale, measure a
temperature which it is metaphysically or epistemically possible for objects to
have. And just as this fact about temperature does not reveal a 'thermal' kind of
possibility, distinct from the metaphysical and epistemic kinds, so the corresponding fact about credences does not show that what they measure is a new
'subjective' kind of possibility.

The fact is that the only possibilities which are relevant here are, as we have
seen, possibilities of truth. And, of such possibilities, what my credence in A
measures would only be a new kind if that kind was subjective, meaning that its
value was whatever I believe it to be. But if that value is just what I take A's
chance or epistemic probability to be, then what is subjective is not the possibility
which this probability measures, but my measure of it. And if that is not what the

value of my credence is, then it is simply my degree of belief in A itself. Admittedly, if this degree is not zero, it will make me believe that A's truth is at least *possible*; but here too that possibility will be metaphysical or epistemic: it is my belief in it that is subjective, not the possibility I thereby believe in.

I conclude therefore that credences do not measure any kind of possibility, even if chances and epistemic probabilities do, and hence that a classical reading of credences cannot be right. This is, however, no objection to the classicism about chance and epistemic probability that we saw in section II to be so plausible. For desirable as a single interpretation of all three kinds of probability may be, it is, as we noted in section I, by no means essential. If the best readings of each kind of probability differ, that need not matter provided that, between them, they can explain how the kinds are linked. This being so, in the rest of this chapter we shall consider the classical view of chances and epistemic probabilities in more detail and on its own merits. Credences, for the present, we may set aside.

IV

Sample Spaces

The classical view of probabilities, as measures of possibility, implies four things. (i) Many possibilities include other possibilities, but some are so-called *ultimate possibilities*, meaning that they include *no* other possibilities. (ii) The probability of any possibility is at least as great as that of any possibility it includes. (This is what makes probability a *measure* of possibilities.) (iii) Any possibility that has a probability includes only finitely many possibilities, and so, in particular, only finitely many ultimate possibilities. (iv) The probability of any possibility is the number of ultimate possibilities it includes, divided by the total number of ultimate possibilities.

To explain these ideas more fully, I shall now introduce some terminology that we shall need again from time to time, using the example of a fair and fairly thrown die. In this terminology, classicism's ultimate possibilities, which in this case we may assume, to start with, are the six possible *results* 1, 2, 3, 4, 5, and 6, are known as *sample points*. These define a so-called *sample space* Ω ('omega'), which is the set {1,2,3,4,5,6}, of all the sample points. Each point has a probability, which I shall write $P[1]$, $P[2]$, etc. (it does not matter here what kind of probabilities these are). All relevant possible *outcomes* of throwing the die can then be represented by *sets* of sample points, i.e. by *subsets* of Ω. So as well as so-called *simple* outcomes like {6}, throwing a six, which contain only one sample point, there are many *complex* outcomes like {1,3,5}, throwing an odd number, {1,2,3}, throwing a number less than 4, etc. The probabilities of all these outcomes, simple or complex, which I shall write $P\{6\}$, $P\{1,2,3\}$, etc., are the sums of the probabilities of the points they contain.

What fixes the probabilities of these sample points and hence of the outcomes that contain them? The classical answer is, as (iv) above says, that the probability of any outcome is proportional to the number of sample points it contains. This is a consequence of the fact that all such points are taken to be *equipossible*, so that that all sample points, and hence all simple outcomes, have the same probability.

This interpretation of probabilities entails several of the basic rules of numerical probability given in chapter 1.VIII. Since necessary outcomes will contain all the sample points in any sample space and impossible ones will contain none, it follows at once that

(1.10)   All necessary propositions have probability 1; and

(1.11)   All impossible propositions have probability 0.

It also follows that

(1.4)   All probabilities lie between 0 and 1 inclusive, i.e.
$0 \leq P(A) \leq 1$; and

(1.5)   The probabilities of A and ¬A always add up to 1, i.e.
$P(A) + P(\neg A) = 1$.

That classicism entails these last two rules may be shown, in sample space terms, as follows. Any proposition A, e.g. that we throw an odd number, has a probability only if it corresponds to an outcome (which where it matters I shall underline: 'A') in some sample space Ω, like the outcome {1,3,5} in the space {1,2,3,4,5,6}. And for A to correspond to some such outcome A, each point in Ω – each possible result – must either make A true or make it false: the points that make A true being those in the outcome A, in this case {1,3,5}, and the ones that make A false being all the rest, namely those in the so-called *complement* of A, written '-A', in this case {2,4,6}.

Then, for holders of the classical theory (or *classicists* for short), A's probability, P(A), is the fraction of Ω's sample points that are in A, a number which therefore cannot be less than 0 or more than 1. This is why, as (1.4) says, all classical probabilities must lie between 0 and 1 inclusive. Similarly, the classical probability of A's negation, ¬A, is the fraction of all Ω's sample points that are in -A, i.e. that are *not* in A. And these two fractions, of the sample points of Ω that are in A, and of those that are not, must add up to 1; which is why, for classicists, P(A) and P(¬A) must, as (1.5) says, do so too.

It is a merit of classicism that it explains these rules of numerical probability; and its doing so also explains why, when classicism was taken for granted, as it was in the eighteenth century, so were these rules. But classicism also has some apparent defects, which we must now consider.

Take the simple outcomes in our die-throwing case: {1}, {2}, {3}, {4}, {5}, {6}. As each of these outcomes contains an equal number – one – of sample points, their classical probabilities are all equal. But if these probabilities are chances, that will be right only if, as we have so far assumed, our die *is* actually fair and fairly thrown. If it is not fair, or is not fairly thrown, then the chances of {1}, {2}, etc. will not all be equal: the chance of {1} may, for example, exceed that of {2}. How can classicism make sense of this?

It can do so by distinguishing different ways of throwing a given number with a die, such as all the different trajectories that make the die land 1. These are now our ultimate possibilities, and – provided they are finite in number – what makes the chance of throwing a 1 greater than the chance of throwing a 2 is the fact that more of these possibilities end up with the die landing 1 than with the die landing 2. So even when two such outcomes do have equal chances, they do so only because they contain equal numbers of trajectories, not because they are themselves simple outcomes.

And as in this case, so in all. For classicism, outcomes with chances that *could* differ from each other cannot all be simple, i.e. contain only one sample point. For as the probability of any outcome in a given sample space is fixed by how many sample points it contains, every simple outcome, which by definition contains just one such point, must be equally probable. This in turn, by making all sample points equally probable, imposes a so-called *uniform probability distribution* on any sample space.

Making all sample points in any given sample space equally probable may look like an arbitrary restriction that empirical evidence could show to be false. But this need not be so, as we can see by comparing it to the idea that time is discrete, with the length of all time intervals fixed by how many temporal quanta – call them 'chronons' – they contain. It is an obvious consequence of this idea that all one-chronon intervals, and therefore all chronons, are equally long. This still lets evidence show that two time intervals specified in other ways are unequal: for on the chronon theory all that such an inequality shows is that the longer interval must contain more chronons. Similarly, for classicists, with the probabilities of outcomes: all that inequalities between them show is that the more probable outcomes must contain more sample points. Classicism's ability to explain unequal probabilities by changing the relevant sample space is not a weakness but a strength.

V

Infinite Sample Spaces

The real problem with measuring time intervals by counting chronons, or possibilities by counting sample points, is that the number of chronons or sample points may be infinite. If it is, then no positive natural number (1, 2, 3, etc.) of chronons or of sample points can measure time intervals or possibilities, and this in particular prevents the probabilities of outcomes being ratios of numbers of sample points. Thus suppose there are infinitely many trajectories by which a thrown die can land 1, land 2, etc., as there may well be. If these trajectories are the sample points, there will be infinitely many of them in any such outcome. It will then make no sense to say, as I did in section IV, that what makes 1 a more probable outcome than 2 is that *more* trajectories make a die land 1 than make it land 2. What then, for classicists, gives the probabilities of outcomes their values?

To see in another case what might do the job, imagine a spinning pointer P, with equal probabilities of stopping within any positive angle of a given size.

This gives P a probability $n/360$ of stopping in any $n°$ angle, and so in particular a probability $1/8$ of stopping in each of the $45°$ angles AOB and BOC shown in Figure 2.

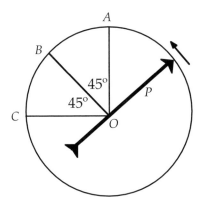

Figure 2: Equal angles within which P has equal probabilities of stopping

In this case, then, instead of a finite probability of P stopping in any precise direction, we have a *probability density distribution*: P's probabilities of stopping are distributed over infinitely many different angles at a density of $1/360$ per degree. What makes this like the classical situation, with equiprobable sample points in a finite sample space, is the fact that this density distribution is *uniform*, i.e. it gives equal probabilities to all outcomes containing equal *ranges* of directions, as measured by the angles they subtend at P's pivot O.

VI

Indifference

If the probabilities of P's stopping are epistemic, this uniform distribution of them may be backed by the so-called *principle of insufficient reason* or (as it has also become known) of *indifference*. This principle says that evidence which gives us no reason to think that any one of a number of mutually exclusive possibilities – like P's stopping within AOB or BOC in Figure 2 – is more probable than any other will give those possibilities equal epistemic probabilities.

Applied to our pointer, the indifference principle says therefore that if, as we assume, our evidence gives us no reason to think P more likely to stop in any one direction than any other, that evidence will give P equal epistemic probabilities of stopping in all equal ranges of directions. So when, as in Figure 2, these ranges are measured by angles, the principle makes our evidence yield the uniform density distribution of epistemic probabilities assumed in section V.

This application of the indifference principle may seem reasonable at first. But as a principle based – as the name '*insufficient* reason' implies – merely on a *lack* of evidence that *P* is more likely to stop in some directions than others, it really will not do. The reason is that it cannot discriminate between different ways of measuring ranges of directions which are equally defensible but do not make the same ranges equal. Thus suppose we measure our ranges of directions not by angles, as in Figure 2, but by how far *P*'s point is from the line *AO*. This can have any orientation, but for illustrative purposes we will suppose it runs north–south, since this would fit a magnetised pointer that is more likely to stop facing north or south than east or west. Now take a point *B'* whose distance from *AO* is half the radius *r* of the circle swept out by *P*'s point, as shown in Figure 3.

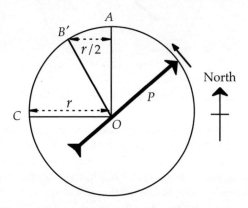

Figure 3: *Un*equal angles within which *P* has equal probabilities of stopping

Then, since by this new measure the range of directions from *A* to *B'* is equal to that from *B'* to *C*, the indifference principle now gives *P* equal probabilities of stopping within the two *unequal* angles *AOB'* and *B'OC*. So if we do not know whether *P* is magnetised or not, we cannot tell which measure to use when applying the principle to derive a uniform probability density distribution.

But does not the measure, and hence the probability distribution, of Figure 3 need justifying by evidence that *P* is biased, i.e. more likely to stop in (say) some 1° angles than in others? Indeed it does, but this does not enable the indifference principle to justify the measure of Figure 2 just because that measure does not favour any angles over any others. The principle could only do that if we knew that *P* is *not* biased, i.e. is *not* more likely to stop in some angles than in others. But evidence which merely fails to identify any such angles does not tell us that *P* is not biased: it simply does not tell us *how* it is biased, if it is. And if our evidence does not tell us whether *P* is biased, let alone how or to what extent, the indifference principle cannot make that evidence favour the density distribution of Figure 2 over that of Figure 3, or indeed over any other distribution of *P*'s probabilities of stopping in various directions.

The inability of the indifference principle to justify unique distributions of epistemic probabilities is not confined to this case, or even to cases where the sample space is infinite. Take our original finite sample space {1,2,3,4,5,6} of the results of throwing a die, and suppose, as the indifference principle requires, that our evidence gives us no reason to think any outcome of a throw more or less probable than any other. So in particular, as our evidence gives us no reason to think the outcome {1,2} more or less likely to occur than not, the indifference principle gives this outcome the epistemic probability, EP{1,2}, the value 1/2. But then, by the same reasoning, it gives an epistemic probability 1/2 to *every* outcome, including {3,4} and {5,6}. But EP{1,2}, EP{3,4} and EP{5,6} cannot *all* be 1/2, or their sum would not be 1, as the rules of numerical probability require, but 1.5. Worse still, since EP{1,2,3,4} = EP{1,2} + EP{3,4}, its being 1/2 implies that EP{3,4} is 0 as well as 1/2, which it cannot be; and similarly for the epistemic probability of every outcome.

Note finally that we cannot save the indifference principle in finite cases by applying it not to all *outcomes* but only to *sample points,* in this case to the results 1, 2, 3, 4, 5 and 6. For as with our pointer *P*, this would only work if we knew that the die was *not* biased, and hence that the set of these results really is a sample space whose points can be identified with the classicist's 'equipossible ultimate possibilities'. But again, evidence which gives us no reason to think any result more likely than any other does not tell us that the die is not biased: it simply does not tell us *how* it is biased, if it is. So if our evidence does not tell us whether it is biased, let alone how, or by how much, the indifference principle cannot make that evidence yield the uniform classical distribution of epistemic probabilities

$$EP\{1\} = EP\{2\} = EP\{3\} = EP\{4\} = EP\{5\} = EP\{6\} = 1/6$$

rather than any other, non-uniform, distribution.

The moral of these two examples, and of the many others that have been used to discredit the indifference principle in the last two centuries, is that epistemic probabilities, equal or unequal, cannot be derived from mere ignorance. The general recognition of this fact has profoundly affected the way in which probability is used to measure how far evidence supports propositions, as we shall see in more detail in chapter 6.

VII

Chances

Meanwhile, we should note that if the indifference principle cannot fix epistemic probabilities, it can certainly not fix chances. For chances, if they exist, are by definition independent of what we do or do not know. The chances, if any, of spun pointers stopping in various angles, of throwing odd numbers with dice, or of radioactive atoms decaying in specified time intervals, are what they are regardless of any evidence we may or may not have about them. However many sample points there are in these sample spaces, we cannot know *a priori* what the chances of these points, or of finite or infinite sets of them, are. For as we saw in section VI, we could not derive this knowledge from the indifference principle even if it applied to chances, which it does not; and no other principle will tell us *a priori* what chance any contingent proposition has of being true.

In particular, since uniform density distributions of chances have no special status, we do not need a privileged measure of ranges of possibilities on which these distributions are uniform. So in the pointer example of section VI, it does not matter whether we use Figure 2's angle measure or Figure 3's distance-from-*AO* measure to give the pointer *P*'s actual chance of stopping in any given range of directions, say in the angle *AOB'* of Figure 3. As this and all other such chances must be the same whichever measure we use to give their density distribution, the different measures will make that distribution look different: if it is uniform on one measure it will not be uniform on the other. But that is immaterial, since it is only the chances which these density distributions yield that matter. The unique values of these chances ensure that their density distribution on either measure of ranges of directions will entail their density distribution on any other measure of those ranges. And because, with chances, it does not matter which measure, if either, makes their density distribution uniform, it does not matter which measure we use.

What then, if not some privileged uniform distribution of chances, fixes the chances of contingent propositions? The best answer, once the indifference principle has been discarded, lies in the link between chances and *frequencies*, such as those with which spun pointers stop in various directions, thrown dice give odd numbers, radioactive atoms decay in various time intervals, and so on. For in these and all other cases, the greater the chance of an outcome of some kind occurring, the more frequently, on the whole, outcomes of that kind are likely to occur.

No one denies that there is some such link between chances and frequencies, and that any view of chance needs to account for it. And the simplest way to do so is to *identify* chances with frequencies, as the so-called *frequency* views of chance do which we shall therefore now discuss in chapter 3. What is less simple, however, is to say *which* frequencies are chances. To that question, as we shall see, different frequency views give very different answers; and some of them even say that what the chances which they identify with frequencies measure are *possibilities*. Classicism's basic idea of probability as a measure of possibility may not be quite dead after all.

Further Reading

The classic source of the classical interpretation of probability is Laplace (1820), chapters II and III. For the terminology of sample spaces, see Feller (1957), chapter I; and for discussions of the distinction drawn in section II between two kinds of conditionals, and of its significance, see the articles in Jackson (1991).

Weaker variants of Laplace's principle of indifference are defended in Keynes (1921), chapter IV, and Kneale (1949), §34. Russell (1948), part V, chapter V, discusses Keynes and indifference. Gillies (2000), chapter 2, discusses Bayes and Keynes on the indifference principle, and the latter's solutions to its paradoxes, as well as the principle's use in physics as a heuristic rather than a valid logical principle. Kneale's views are discussed by Blackburn (1973), who defends a version of the indifference principle to warrant certain short-term predictions.

3
Frequencies

I

Credences

Recognition of the defects of classicism outlined in chapter 2 led in the nineteenth century to a quite different interpretation of probabilities, as *frequencies*. This, in the coin-tossing case, takes the probability of tosses landing heads to measure not the possibility of that outcome on *one* toss but how often it occurs on *many* tosses. On this view the probability of heads is not the fraction of possible trajectories on which the toss lands heads but the so-called *relative frequency* of heads, i.e. the fraction of tosses that do land heads.

The frequency view, or *frequentism* for short, does not, however, apply to all kinds of probability. In particular, like classicism, it does not apply to credences. We saw in chapter 2.III that credences do not measure a distinct subjective kind of possibility. Nor are they a distinct subjective kind of frequency. For suppose my credence in some coin tosses landing heads is 1/2. This credence may indeed derive from my belief that their chance of landing heads is 1/2, a chance which frequentists identify with the relative frequency of heads on those tosses. But, as we saw in 2.III, this derivation does not make my credence a kind of chance, and still less does it make it a kind of frequency. It does not for example mean that half the time I believe these coin tosses will land heads and half the time believe they will not. To have a credence 1/2 in heads is not to have a degree of belief which oscillates between 1 and 0, but rather to have a steady intermediate degree of belief, whose probability measure is half way between 1 and 0.

Frequentists who wish to apply their view to probabilities of all kinds might therefore deny that credences exist. That is, they might deny either that belief comes by degrees at all or that, if it does, those degrees have a probability measure. But this would be unreasonable. The case for credences to be given in chapter 5 does not require them to be frequencies; and the case for a frequency view of other kinds of probability does not require it to apply to credences. Chances and epistemic probabilities may be frequencies even if credences are not. So just as classical readings of those kinds of probability were assessed on their own merits in chapter 2, frequency readings of them will now be considered in the same way, starting with epistemic probabilities.

II

Epistemic Probabilities

Take the proposition that the result of throwing a die is an even number, i.e. that {2,4,6} is an outcome of the throw. What on the frequency view is the epistemic probability, given that proposition, that the result is a 4, i.e. that {4} is also an outcome of this throw? The obvious answer is that this epistemic probability, EP({4} | {2,4,6}), is the relative frequency of {4} outcomes among {2,4,6} outcomes.

So far, seemingly so good. Better still, now consider the epistemic probability, EP({4} | {1,2,3,4,5,6}), of a {4} outcome given that {1,2,3,4,5,6} is an outcome. Given that all throws land 1, 2, 3, 4, 5 or 6, this is just the epistemic probability of throwing a 4 given the minimal evidence that a die *is* thrown. So this probability, for frequentists, is the relative frequency of fours among *all* throws. But on the frequency view it is also the *chance* of throwing a 4. Frequentism seems therefore to promise a unified account of chance and epistemic probability by realising a possibility mooted in chapter 1.I, that of making chances a subset of epistemic probabilities.

This promise, however, is illusory, because the frequency view does not make sense of *enough* epistemic probabilities. To see why not we must look more closely at what, on the frequency view, can *have* probabilities. Take the case of coin tosses landing heads. What can happen more or less frequently is not that a *single* coin toss lands heads but that members of some *class* of tosses land heads. This class is what frequentists call a *reference class*, to which all frequency probabilities are relative. For frequentists, then, most epistemic probabilities are not features of so-called *singular* propositions, like the proposition that a specific toss lands heads. They are relations between instances of two different properties, like that of being a coin toss and that of landing heads, the relation being the fraction of instances of the former which are also instances of the latter.

The trouble for frequentism is that too many epistemic probabilities *are* probabilities of singular propositions. These probabilities are indeed relations, as frequencies are, but rarely ones with which frequencies with the right values can be identified. Thus suppose in our die-throwing example that the epistemic probability EP({4} | {2,4,6}) relates the proposition A that a *specific* throw lands 4 to the proposition B that it lands 2, 4 or 6. Then since A, like the proposition that a single coin toss lands heads, is a singular proposition about a specific event, the relevant reference class of throws that land 2, 4 or 6 has this one throw as its only member, so that the frequency of fours in it can only be 1 (if the throw lands 4) or 0 (if it does not). But neither 1 nor 0 is a credible value of EP(A | B), which if the throw is unbiased will be 1/3 and which, even if the throw is biased but not to either extreme, will still be less than 1 and more than 0.

What can frequentists say about this? They seem to have two options. One is to deny that there is any such thing as the epistemic probability of an outcome of a single throw; the other is to say that there is such a thing, and that its value is equal to the relative frequency of that outcome on many such throws. Which should they say?

For present purposes it does not matter, since both responses deny that the frequency interpretation applies to $EP(A \mid B)$ itself. If the first response denies this explicitly, the second does so implicitly by making $EP(A \mid B)$ equal in value to a *different* frequency, that of the outcome {4} on *other* throws of which {2,4,6} is an outcome.

To show that this equality of values does not support a frequency reading of $EP(A \mid B)$ itself, I must digress to stress an important general distinction between *identifying* two apparently different quantities and equating their *values*. I drew this distinction in chapter 2.III and again in section I above in distinguishing a coin toss's chance $CH(H)$ of landing heads from my credence $CR(H)$ that it will do so. For even if both of these are $1/2$ – and even if my $CR(H)$ is $1/2$ because I think this $CH(H)$ is $1/2$ – they are not the same thing: chances of coin tosses landing heads are properties of those tosses; credences in coin tosses landing heads are properties of people. So coin tosses having a chance $CH(H)$ and my having a credence $CR(H)$ are quite different facts, as is shown by the fact that either can exist without the other. Take coins tossed by an automatic device which no one watches: those coin tosses may have a $CH(H) = 1/2$ without anyone knowing about them and therefore without anyone having any credence $CR(H)$ in their landing heads. Conversely, I can have a $CR(H)$ in some other coins landing heads even if no $CH(H)$ exists, perhaps because, for example, unknown to me, those coins are never actually tossed.

As for chances and credences, so for chances and epistemic probabilities. To see this, let H be the proposition that a specific coin toss lands heads, and E be the proposition that its chance of doing so, $CH(H)$, is p, where p's value depends on whether, which way and to what extent the toss is biased. Then however we interpret chances and epistemic probabilities, we can all agree that $EP(H \mid E)$, the epistemic probability of heads on *this* toss, relative to the proposition E that *its* chance of landing heads is p, is also p. Yet this equality of their values does nothing to show that $EP(H \mid E)$ and $CH(H)$ are the same thing; and they are not, since $EP(H \mid E)$, like my $CR(H)$, can exist even if $CH(H)$ does not, for the following quite general reason.

The reason is that for no propositions A and B does the existence of $EP(A \mid B)$, whatever its value, entail that B is *true*. For the fact, if it is a fact, that $EP(A \mid B) = p$, for some p between 1 and 0, links the propositions A and B whether they are true or not – just as entailment, for example, when it links two propositions, links them whether or not they are true. Consequently, just as B need not be true for the disjunction $A \vee B$ to be entailed by it, so B need not be true for A to have an epistemic probability conditional on it. So, in our coin-tossing case, $EP(H \mid E)$ can exist and have a specific value p even if E is false, either because $CH(H)$ actually has some value other than p or because, as before, $CH(H)$ does not even exist, since no coins are actually tossed.

We shall see later, in chapter 6, just how similar to entailment epistemic probability is. Here we need only note that if epistemic probabilities exist, then whatever they are, they are not frequencies. For, to revert to our die-throwing example, once we distinguish identity from sameness of values, we can see that *no* frequencies can be identified with the epistemic probability EP(A|B) that a specific throw lands 4 (A), given that it lands 2, 4 or 6 (B). We have seen already that this EP(A|B) cannot be identified with the only frequency whose value it might equal, that of {4} outcomes among all throws with {2,4,6} outcomes. It can also not be the frequency, 1 or 0, of a {4} outcome on this particular throw: and not just because, as we said earlier, its value need not be 1 or 0; but also because, as we can now see, its existence entails neither that {2,4,6} *is* an outcome of this throw nor even that the throw occurs. And if neither of these two frequencies can be identified with this particular EP(A|B), then certainly no other frequency can.

III

Humean Chances

If the epistemic probabilities of outcomes of a single throw of a die or toss of a coin cannot be frequencies, how can their chances be frequencies? Take the chance CH(H) of one coin toss landing heads. As before, the frequency of heads on this toss can only be 1, if the coin lands heads, or 0, if it does not. Yet these are not the only possible values of CH(H). Why is this not as serious an objection to frequentism about chance as it is to frequentism about epistemic probability?

The answer is that it is easier to deny the existence of so-called *single-case* chances, like the chance of heads on a single coin toss, than the existence of their epistemic counterparts. I remarked in section II that frequentists might deny the latter, but did not then pursue that idea, simply because if epistemic probabilities exist at all, then propositions like 'This coin toss lands heads' must surely have them. And these propositions include not just trivial ones, about the outcomes of tossing coins and throwing dice, but serious scientific, forensic, legal and clinical examples like those we gave in chapter 1: 'Our universe had a beginning', 'The butler did it', 'The defendant is innocent', 'This patient has flu', and so on. It is as hard to deny that evidence can give these propositions epistemic probabilities as it is to identify those probabilities with frequencies.

Not so with the *chances* of propositions like 'This coin toss will land heads', 'This radium atom will decay within a year', 'Their next child will be a girl', 'The Rembrandt will be stolen', 'You will live to be a hundred'. It may not be easy to deny that these propositions have chances, but it may have to be done if our best theory of what chances are both requires it and provides credible surrogates for those chances. That is what I think frequentists must show.

However, before considering how they might show it, we should see how akin frequentism is to what I shall call a Humean view of causation (even though Hume himself may not have held it, and other views have also been called 'Humean'). On the view I have in mind, causation does not really link singular causes, like a specific tossing of a coin, to singular effects, like the coin's landing. That is to say, such effects need not be made inevitable by any 'necessary connections' between them and their causes, nor by any intrinsic 'causal powers' which those causes possess. Holders of this Humean view will deny that any such connections or powers need be invoked to justify calling causes *sufficient* for their effects. For them, all it takes in reality to make tossing a coin a sufficient cause of its landing is that, in the relevant circumstances (in the air, over land, under gravity, etc.), tossed coins *always* land.

Similarly with causes that are said to be *necessary* for their effects in the sense that, without them, those effects will not occur. Here too our Humeans will deny that any 'occult' connections or powers are needed to make sense of the idea that the absence of such causes stops their effects occurring. In their view all it takes to make tossing a coin a necessary cause of its landing is that in the circumstances (e.g. where coins only move if they are tossed) *only* tossed coins land.

But how can this view of causation explain how sufficient causes are thought to *necessitate* their effects by giving them no – i.e. zero – chance of not occurring? If chances are frequencies the answer is easy. For if sufficient causes are those that are *always* accompanied by their effects, then the relative frequency with which they are *not* so accompanied will be zero. And for frequentists this is all that a zero chance is: a zero relative frequency. Thus frequentism about chance gives a simple Humean reading of the idea that a sufficient cause necessitates its effects by giving them zero chances of not occurring: for all this need amount to in reality is that effects always accompany their sufficient causes.

Similarly with the idea that an effect *cannot* occur unless its necessary causes occur, meaning that without these causes it has no – zero – chance of occurring. Here again frequentism provides a simple Humean reading of this supposed necessity. For if effects *never* occur in the absence of their necessary causes, then the relative frequency, and hence for frequentists the chance, of their occurrence will be zero.

And as with causation, so with laws of nature. Suppose all human beings, past, present and future, are mortal. On some views of laws, this general fact will only be a law and not a mere 'cosmic coincidence' if everyone's humanity makes his or her eventual death *necessary* in some sense which (to distinguish it from logical necessity) is often called *nomic* or *natural*. However, our Humeans can reject any such non-logical notion of natural necessity. They can take laws to be merely a subset of cosmic coincidences, such as those postulated or explained by true scientific theories. And if their opponents identify the natural necessity of our mortality (say) with the fact that

all humans have a chance 1 of being mortal,

then our Humeans can use the frequency view of chance to reduce this to the simple general fact that

all humans are mortal.

If frequentism about chances supports this Humean view of laws, support also goes the other way. For as I hinted at the end of chapter 2, frequentists cannot credibly claim that *all* frequencies are chances. Take the fact that six of the nine major planets have orbits that are further from the sun than is the earth's. No one will infer from this that major planets have a 2/3 chance of being further from the sun than we are. Frequentists must therefore distinguish frequencies that are chances from frequencies that are not. And with all the chances postulated by modern science, such as those listed in chapter 1.II, a Humean view of the statistical laws they occur in may well provide frequentists with the distinction they need. For whatever criterion Humeans use to distinguish between statistical laws and mere statistical coincidences, frequentists may also be able to use it to distinguish chances from other frequencies in the very same way.

Take for example the theory of radioactive decay, which says that

radium atoms have a chance p_t of decaying within t years

and hence, on a frequency view of chance, that

the frequency of radium atoms decaying within t years is p_t,

where p_t is a function of t that usually increases (and can never decrease) with t, since all atoms which decay within *less* than t years also decay within t years. Suppose all this is so, and suppose also that what makes this statistical fact a law is its place in a true theory of microphysics. This, frequentists may then say, is what makes the relative frequency of radium atoms decaying within any given time interval a chance, which the relative frequency of planets further from the sun than we are is not.

Note, however, that this view of laws and chances requires a sharp distinction between so-called *deterministic* laws, like the law that all humans are mortal, and *statistical* laws, like those of radioactivity. Simple examples of the former can be stated by universal generalisations like 'All humans are mortal', of the form

(3.1) $\forall x (Fx \rightarrow Gx)$,

where '$\forall x$' means 'for all x', '_ $\rightarrow$ ...' means 'if _ then ...' and 'Fx' and 'Gx' in our example mean respectively that x is human and that x is mortal. Statistical laws, by contrast, cannot be stated in that way on this view of laws and chances. For suppose we stated the law of radium's decay in the same form, as

(3.2) $\forall x (Rx \rightarrow \text{CH}(D_t x)=p_t)$,

where 'Rx' means that x is a radium atom and '$D_t x$' means that x decays within t years. Then if a is a specific radium atom, it follows that

$Ra \rightarrow \text{CH}(D_t a)=p_t$

and hence, since 'Ra' is true, that

$\text{CH}(D_t a)=p_t$;

i.e. that the individual atom a has a chance p_t of decaying within t years.

But for frequentists there is no such thing as a chance p_t (other than 1 or 0) of a single atom decaying in a given period of t years. Such a chance, in their view, is no more a property of a single atom than, for example, the property of being *numerous* is. Just as the latter is a property of *all* atoms but not of any one of them, so is the relative frequency of radium atoms decaying within t years. So on the frequency view, simple statistical laws should be stated as instances not of (3.1) but of something like

(3.3) $f(Gx/Fx) = p,$

where $f(Gx/Fx)$ is the relative frequency among F-things of those that are G. In this notation the right way for frequentists to state our law of radioactivity is as

(3.4) $f_t(D_t x/Rx) = p_t,$

where $f_t(D_t x/Rx)$ is the relative frequency among radium atoms of those that decay within t years.

It is debatable whether the probabilistic laws of modern science really differ from their deterministic predecessors in the way that (3.3) and (3.1) imply. It is not for example obvious that, as (3.4) implies, the laws of radioactivity tell us nothing about a single atom's prospects of decay, or that epidemiologists can tell me nothing about *my* chance of catching flu when exposed to it. It is thus not clear whether this consequence of the frequency view of chance counts for or against it. If it counts against it, that fact may favour the interpretations of chance we shall discuss in chapter 4, which differ from frequentism in this very respect. But first we must examine frequentism in a little more detail.

IV

Frequentism and Classicism

Let us start by comparing the frequency view of chances with the classical view. We saw in section III how combining frequentism with a Humean view of causation and of laws handles ideas of causal and natural necessity. It does so, as we saw, by substituting for the so-called *modal* notions of necessity and possibility which these ideas invoke the following non-modal surrogates:

> what is *necessary* → what *always* happens;
> what is *impossible* → what *never* happens;
> what is *possible* → what *sometimes* happens.

And if we think that *possibility*, unlike necessity and impossibility, comes by degrees, frequentism offers us a surrogate for that too:

> *how possible* something is → *how frequently* it happens.

In this way frequentism provides a non-modal surrogate for classicism's idea of chance as a measure of physical possibility. By so doing, it explains the appeal of this idea while denying that reality need contain anything that does not actually exist or happen.

I must stress at this point that frequentist surrogates for classical possibilities are just that: surrogates. Frequentism does not explain possibilities: it explains them away. This is evident in frequency readings of the outcomes of throwing a die. These readings may still represent those outcomes as sets of sample points in a sample space {1,2,3,4,5,6} of possible results. But these points need not now be 'ultimate' in the sense of chapter 2.IV, since frequentists do not take an outcome's probability to be fixed by the sample points it contains. A frequentist's sample space may be *any* suitable set of exhaustive and exclusive alternatives. So while the most natural space for throws of a die may still be {1,2,3,4,5,6}, it might just as well be {1-2,3-4,5-6}, {odds,evens} or any other set of exhaustive and exclusive results of throwing a die.

Moreover, as the number of an outcome's sample points fixes its classical but not its frequency probability, these probabilities may differ. This means that two outcomes may have the same classical probability but different frequencies, or *vice versa*. Thus the frequency of {1,3,5} may exceed that of {2,4,6} and equal that of {1,2}. Still, as we explained in chapter 2.IV, classical probabilities can always be adjusted to fit frequency data by changing the sample space, in this case from the set {1,2,3,4,5,6} of results to a larger set of trajectories, more of which can then be taken to lead to odd numbers turning up than to even ones doing so. Apparent conflicts between classical and frequency probabilities can always be resolved in this way.

Note however that it will always be the classical probability that has to be altered to fit the frequency, not the other way round. The reason lies in the obstacles we saw in chapter 2 to fixing classical probabilities, especially in infinite sample spaces. Frequentists, by contrast, face no such obstacles, and in particular need not make uniform chance distributions basic. So they need not give the spun pointer P in chapter 2 a uniform distribution over any natural measure of the directions in which P may stop: P's chance of stopping in any range of directions is simply the frequency with which, when spun often, it does stop in that range. Frequentism thus evades all the problems posed for classicism by infinities of sample points and by rival measures of ranges of them.

If frequentism does better than classicism in these respects, it also matches it by entailing and thereby explaining the same rules of numerical probability. Only here what explains the fact that

(1.10) All necessary propositions have probability 1; and

(1.11) All impossible propositions have probability 0,

is the fact that what *must* happen on any one occasion will *always* happen, and that what *cannot* happen on any one occasion will *never* happen.

To see how frequentism entails

(1.4) All probabilities lie between 0 and 1 inclusive, i.e.
$$0 \leq P(A) \leq 1$$

we must take account of the fact, noted in section II, that this view makes probabilities relations between instances of two properties, like the properties of landing heads and of being a toss of a coin. Here therefore, in the notation of (3.2) above, we may take $P(A)$ to be the relative frequency $f(Gx/Fx)$ among F-things (e.g. coin tosses) of those that are also G (land heads). Then the reason why, for frequentists, all probabilities lie between 1 and 0 is simply that, for any F and G, the number of F-things that are G can be neither greater than the total number of F-things nor less than 0.

Similarly, the reason frequentism entails

(1.5) The probabilities of A and ¬A always add up to 1, i.e.
$$P(A) + P(\neg A) = 1,$$

is that because, for any F and G, the number of F-things that *are* G plus the number that are *not* G equals the total number of F-things,

$$f(Gx/Fx) + f(\neg Gx/Fx) = 1.$$

So far so good for frequentism. Yet not far enough to make it an all-purpose interpretation of probability. For as we saw in section I, frequentism does not apply to credences, any more than classicism does. But neither, as we saw in section II, does it apply to epistemic probabilities, to which classicism does apply. And even as a view of chance, frequentism faces problems, as we shall now see.

V

Limiting Frequencies

Infinities pose the main problem for frequentism, as they do for classicism. Only here the problem is generated not by infinite sample spaces – frequentists, as we have seen, have no trouble with these – but by infinite reference classes, in which only frequencies of 0 and 1 are defined. Thus while, for example, infinitely many coin tosses yielding only finitely many heads makes the frequency of heads 0 (since n/∞, if defined at all, is 0 for all finite n) and arguably that of tails 1, no other frequency makes sense (since ∞/∞ is not defined).

This is a serious problem for frequentism, since some real reference classes are infinite. Take the chance of radium atoms decaying within a millennium. Even if the number of atoms is finite, there are infinitely many 1000-year time intervals, because a new one starts every instant. So the reference class here is infinite, because for each atom there is an infinity of 1000-year intervals, each starting at a different moment, within which that atom may or may not decay. But then there is no such thing as the frequency of radium atoms decaying within 1000 years, and so apparently no such thing, for frequentists, as the chance of their doing so.

To this problem two frequentist solutions have been proposed. One is to deny the existence of infinite reference classes, or at least to ignore them. For even if there are such classes, they must contain finite sub-classes: so why not identify chances with relative frequencies in those?

There are three difficulties with this solution. One is that it violates the rule that a chance should always be identified with the *largest* relevant reference class. If for example we tossed our coin 1000 times, we would surely identify its chance of landing heads with the frequency of heads in that 1000-membered reference class, not in any smaller sub-class. This rule also holds in less artificial cases, like our chances of catching flu when exposed to it. We may indeed distinguish the chances of catching flu in different populations, like various age groups, or those who have been vaccinated and those who have not. But for each such population the right reference class is still that of *all* its members. Certainly it is with the frequencies of outcomes in just such *maximal* classes that statisticians generally identify chances in given populations.

The second difficulty is how to justify excluding some members of a maximal reference class, a difficulty that will be especially acute if the class is infinite, for then infinitely many members must be excluded to yield a finite class.

The third difficulty is that, even if we could justify excluding members of a maximal reference class, there is no obvious way of deciding which members to exclude. Yet some way there must be, because different sub-classes may yield different frequencies, only one of which can be identified with a corresponding chance.

For these reasons most frequentists have adopted a quite different solution to the problem of infinite reference classes. This solution starts from the idea of a *limit of a sequence*. Take the following sequence of numbers:

Sequence of positions:	A	B	C	D	...
Sequence of numbers:	1.1	1.01	1.001	1.0001	...

This sequence of numbers has a limit: 1. More precisely, all the numbers in it after position A differ from 1 by less than 0.1, after position B by less than 0.01, and so on. So for any positive number δ, however small, there is a position after which all numbers differ from 1 by less than δ. That is what makes 1 the limit of this sequence of numbers.

Now imagine a sequence of ever larger but always finite classes of n radium atoms, and suppose the numbers m, and thus the relative frequencies $f_n = m/n$, of those that decay within 1000 years of a given moment, happen to be as follows:

Sequence of positions:	A	B	C	D	...
Number n of atoms:	10	100	1000	10,000	...
Number m that decay:	2	34	301	3145	...
Sequence of $f_n = m/n$:	0.2	0.34	0.301	0.3145	...

Then this sequence of frequencies may also have a limit f_∞, called its *limiting frequency*. That is, there may be a number f_∞ such that, for any positive number δ, however small, there is a position in the sequence after which all the frequencies differ from f_∞ by less than δ. If there is, then on the *limiting frequency view* of chance, f_∞ is the chance of radium atoms decaying within 1000 years.

Several points need making about this limiting frequency view. First, since the sequence it relies on is empirical, and not generated by a mathematical rule as our first sequence was, its limit f_∞ cannot be *proved* to exist. So the mere fact that some but not all radium atoms decay within 1000 years does not entail, on this view, that they have a chance of doing so. If they do, that is an extra fact about them.

Second, the limiting frequency view does not take *all* limiting frequencies to be chances. To see why not, imagine a coin, tossed for ever, landing heads (H) and tails (T) alternately, thus generating the following sequence:

Number n of tosses:	1	2	3	4	5	6	7	8	...
Result of nth toss:	H	T	H	T	H	T	H	T	...
Number m of heads:	1	1	2	2	3	3	4	4	...
Sequence of $f_n(H) = m/n$:	1	1/2	2/3	1/2	3/5	1/2	4/7	1/2	...

Then although this sequence of frequencies *has* a limit – 1/2 – no one would take all these tosses to have a 0.5 chance of landing heads. (If they have any such chance, it presumably alternates between 1 and 0.) This suggests that a limiting frequency will only be a chance if most if not all *sub*-sequences of the sequence (e.g. every alternate toss) have the same limiting frequency as the whole sequence, a condition that is met in the radium case but not here. This principle is sometimes called that of *the impossibility of gambling systems*, since it says that no way of selecting tosses to bet on (e.g. 'only bet on heads after tails') will change a gambler's chance of success.

The no-gambling-system principle is, however, hard to state properly, since in no interesting sequence (as opposed say to 1,1,1,1, . . .) will *all* sub-sequences have the same limit: think for example of the sub-sequence of those radium atoms that *do* decay in 1000 years. And requiring only 'arbitrary' or 'randomly chosen' sub-sequences to have the same limit raises the question of how to define 'arbitrary' or 'random' without vicious circularity. Whether this can be done by a frequency view is a moot point; but here I shall assume that it can, since all chances interpreted as limiting frequencies must certainly satisfy some such principle.

VI

Hypothetical Frequencies

If infinite reference classes pose one problem for frequentism, finite ones pose another. The problem is one noted at the start of section III: the fact that the frequency $f_1(H)$ of heads on a single coin toss can only be 1, if the toss lands heads, or 0, if it does not. So for frequentists no single toss can, as such, have a chance of heads other than 1 or 0. All other chances of heads must be relative to larger reference classes. But even then their values will be limited: to 0, 1/2 or 1 in a class of two tosses; to 0, 1/3, 2/3 or 1 in a class of three; and so on. Only a very large reference class can enable chances to have many of the values between 0 and 1. This provides another reason for the rule mentioned in section V, that all chances should be identified with frequencies in *maximal* reference classes.

That rule however merely minimises the problem: it does not solve it. If a coin *is* only tossed once, the maximal reference class will have only one member and the frequency of heads in it can only be 1 or 0. And if there are only finitely many tosses, then however many there are, there will be many theoretically possible chances of heads that cannot be identified with any actual frequency of heads.

This is a very unattractive consequence of the frequency view: what chances a coin could have of landing heads when tossed should not depend on how often it happens to be tossed. So why not identify CH(H) with a *hypothetical* frequency, i.e. with how frequently the coin *would* land heads if it *were* tossed more often? The question then is '*how* often?', to which the limiting frequency view enables the only non-arbitrary answer, namely 'infinitely often'.

This is the third version of frequentism (the first two being the finite and the limiting actual-frequency views given above): chances are *hypothetical limiting frequencies*. It overcomes several objections to the other versions; but it faces one large question of its own: what fixes the frequencies, or limiting frequencies, in hypothetical classes? Suppose for example the chance CH(H) of a coin toss landing heads is 1/2: what on this view gives this chance that value? It cannot be any actual frequency, even if there is one, since landing heads on half of six – or of six trillion – actual tosses is consistent with *any* limiting frequency of heads in an infinity of hypothetical tosses. Nor is 1/2 the only *possible* limit: for as heads and tails are both possible outcomes of any one toss, the limiting frequency of heads *could* take any value from 0 to 1 inclusive. What then, on this view, makes CH(H) = 1/2?

To see the answer to this question we must distinguish what *could* happen in a hypothetical situation from what *would* happen in it. It is true that if our coin were tossed for ever, the limiting frequency $f_\infty(H)$ of heads could be anything from 0 to 1. But the hypothetical limiting frequency view need not deny this: it need only insist that, while $f_\infty(H)$ *could* be anything, it *would* in fact be 1/2. There is no contradiction here, any more than there is in my saying that while I could go by bus if I went to London today, I would in fact go by train. But just as this does not tell us what, when I do not go to London, makes it true that if I did I would go by train, so we may still want to know what, when our coin is not tossed for ever, makes it true that, if it were, $f_\infty(H)$ would be 1/2. To that question there are several possible answers, which we shall consider in chapter 4.

Further Reading

Classic frequency interpretations of probability are given by Reichenbach (1949), and von Mises (1957). Russell (1948), part V, expounds and comments on the finite frequency theory (in chapter III) and Reichenbach's theory (in chapter IV). Gillies (2000), chapter 5, discusses von Mises's theory with a historical background. Howson and Urbach (1993), chapter 9, also discusses von Mises's theory and offers a Bayesian reconstruction of it (see chapter 10 below). For Humean chances, see Lewis (1994), reprinted as chapter 15 of his (1999): this uses frequencies to develop a view of single-case chances, compatible with Humean supervenience.

For causation, see the papers in Sosa and Tooley (1993), especially Salmon (1980), and Lewis (1973a), which is reprinted, with a postscript on indeterministic causation, in his (1986). For a more detailed Humean theory of causation, see

Mackie (1974), and for a non-Humean theory see Tooley (1987). For a more detailed probabilistic view of causation, see my (1995), especially chapters 5–8, where I argue that causes must raise the chances of their effects. For Humean views of laws of nature, see Ayer (1956) and chapter 3.3 of Lewis (1973b); for a non-Humean view, see Armstrong (1983).

4
Possibilities and Propensities

I

Modal Chances

The classical interpretation of chapter 2 took chances, like the chance CH(H) of a coin toss landing heads, to measure possibilities that are contingent, quantitative and – in the sense explained in 2.II – metaphysical rather than epistemic. Moreover, since these possibilities include the possible truth of singular propositions like 'This coin toss lands heads', this view lets a CH(H) whose value is p, where $0<p<1$, be what in chapter 3.III I called a *single-case* chance, which on the frequency views of chapter 3 it cannot be.

This classical reading of chance requires the possibilities it postulates to exist, sand to have a measure that satisfies the rules of numerical probability. To this basic assumption it then adds the claim that the value p of a single-case chance like CH(H) is equal to the fraction of all the 'ultimate possibilities' – e.g. the coin's possible trajectories when tossed – which result in the outcome with that chance.

All the objections to classicism raised in chapter 2 are to this extra claim, that possibilities are measured by how many ultimate possibilities they contain. We may deny this while still accepting that single-case chances like CH(H) measure contingent metaphysical possibilities (which are what I shall mean here by 'possibilities'). This basic idea I shall call the *modal view* of chance, and chances so understood I shall call *modal chances*. And one reason to adopt this view is the answer it lets us give to the question, raised at the end of chapter 3, of what makes it true that, if a coin were tossed for ever, the limiting frequency of heads would be 1/2.

The answer rests on what I shall call the *modality-to-frequency* assumption (MF): that any repeatable outcome with any degree of possibility p has a hypothetical limiting frequency that increases with p (with one exception, dealt with in section VI). More precisely, in the notation of (3.2), for any F, F', G and G', where the possibility of any F-thing's being G is p, and of any F'-thing's being G' is p',

(MF) If p is at least as great as p', then $f_\infty(Gx/Fx) \geq f_\infty(G'x/F'x)$.

Assuming (MF), we may take a modal chance to be a metaphysical possibility measured by the hypothetical limiting frequency which it entails.

One apparent example of this modal view is the so-called *ergodic hypothesis* of statistical mechanics as applied to objects like gases whose macroscopic states (e.g. their temperatures) depend on their microscopic states (e.g. the kinetic energies of their molecules). Of any such object or system the ergodic hypothesis says that, if it stayed long enough in any one macrostate T, it would be

(i)   in each *possible* microstate compatible with T at some time, and
(ii) in any given set of those states for a length of time proportional to *a probability measure of that set*. (Sklar 1993, pp. 159–60)

To see how this hypothesis can link possibilities to hypothetical limiting frequencies, suppose gases are made up of randomly moving molecules forming a system that may at any instant be in any one of many incompatible microstates, defined (say) by the different fractions of the gas's molecules that have given velocities and hence kinetic energies at that instant.

Then to see how (MF) makes the ergodic hypothesis apply to such a system, imagine a gas g with just four molecules. Imagine also, for simplicity, that these molecules can only have a kinetic energy (KE) of 0, 1 or 2 units each and a mean KE of 1 unit (corresponding to a fixed gas temperature T). The gas system g may then be in any one of the three possible microstates A, B and C shown in Table 1:

Possible microstate of gas g	A	B	C
No. of molecules with KE $= 0$	0	1	2
No. of molecules with KE $= 1$	4	2	0
No. of molecules with KE $= 2$	0	1	2
Mean KE of molecules	1	1	1

Table 1

To apply (MF) to g, assume first that g is at a constant temperature T throughout a time interval of length t. Next, assume that during this time g is, at random, in the microstates A, B and C for periods of time totalling t_A, t_B and t_C, so that $t_A + t_B + t_C = t$. Then the frequencies with which, during t, g actually is in the three states A, B and C are respectively

$$t_A/t, \ t_B/t \text{ and } t_C/t.$$

This makes the limits, if any, of these three fractions as $t \to \infty$, i.e.

$$f_\infty(t_A/t), f_\infty(t_B/t) \text{ and } f_\infty(t_C/t),$$

the limiting frequencies

$$f_\infty(Ag), f_\infty(Bg) \text{ and } f_\infty(Cg)$$

with which g *would* be in the states A, B and C if it remained for ever at the temperature T.

Now take $\text{CH}(Ag)$, $\text{CH}(Bg)$ and $\text{CH}(Cg)$ to be g's modal chances of being A, B and C at any instant within the interval t, i.e. to be probability measures of the metaphysical possibilities that at any such instant g actually is A, B or C. Then if these chances are not zero, it follows from (MF) and our assumptions about g that, as the ergodic hypothesis says,

(i)   in a sufficiently long run, g will be in each of the states A, B and C at some time or other; and

(ii) the hypothetical limiting frequencies $f_\infty(Ag)$, $f_\infty(Bg)$ and $f_\infty(Cg)$ exist and their values are those of $CH(Ag)$, $CH(Bg)$ and $CH(Cg)$.

Finally, let us ask if this imaginary instance of the ergodic hypothesis not only exemplifies (MF) but also supports the full classical reading of the modal chances involved. Does it, in other words, require $CH(Ag)$, $CH(Bg)$ and $CH(Cg)$ to be fixed by the fractions of 'ultimate possibilities' contained in Ag, Bg and Cg?

To see that it does not, suppose first that A, B and C are basic properties of the system g, i.e. points in its so-called *state space* $\{A,B,C\}$. This makes Ag, Bg and Cg sample points of the sample space $\{Ag,Bg,Cg\}$ and hence the system g's ultimate possibilities. For classicists this entails the chance distribution

(D1) $CH(Ag) = CH(Bg) = CH(Cg) = 1/3$.

In fact however Ag, Bg and Cg are *not* ultimate possibilities of the system g as described. For just as we saw in chapter 2.IV that the many possible trajectories of a thrown die provide many different ways in which the die can land 1, 2, 3, etc., so g's four molecules provide many different ways in which g can be A, B or C. More to the present point, they provide more ways of being in some of these states than in others. Thus, while g has only *one* way of being A (with all four molecules having KE = 1), it has – as readers may work out for themselves – *twelve* ways of being B and *six* ways of being C. So if these nineteen ways of having a mean KE = 1 are the sample points of our sample space, the classical view gives us the chance distribution

(D2) $CH(Ag) = 1/19$; $CH(Bg) = 12/19$; $CH(Cg) = 6/19$.

Which is right: (D1) or (D2)? We cannot tell *a priori*, not even if we could know *a priori* which are the sample points of this particular sample space. For as we saw in chapter 2.VII, we cannot know *a priori* that even the sample points of a sample space have equal chances. A theory may say that they do, but whether that theory is right is an empirical matter, answerable in this case, via the ergodic hypothesis, to estimates of how long g actually spends in the states A, B and C. So while our specimen of the ergodic hypothesis does indeed follow from our modal view of chance, it gives no support to the extra claims of the classical view.

I should emphasise here that the appeal of modal chances does not depend on the truth of the ergodic hypothesis as stated above. That hypothesis merely illustrates the general thesis (MF) linking the basic modal idea, that chances measure metaphysical possibilities, to the idea that they entail hypothetical limiting frequencies. And where (MF) holds I think it improves both ideas.

Take for example the law of radioactive decay discussed in chapter 3.III. By crediting each radium atom with a contingent and quantitative metaphysical possibility of decaying within any period of t years, the modal view allows this and other such laws to have the form (3.1) of a simple deterministic law, rather than the distinct and debatable statistical form (3.3). By so doing the view also both explains why a hypothetical limiting frequency of radium atoms decaying within t years exists, and enables that frequency to be a probability measure of the metaphysical possibility which entails it.

Yet however attractive modal chances may seem, they come at what many philosophers will consider a metaphysically exorbitant price: the acceptance of metaphysical possibilities which currently orthodox theories of possible worlds cannot accommodate. To see why not, we must look again at the possible-world semantics sketched in chapter 2.II for conditionals like

(2.2) 'If Oswald had not killed Kennedy, someone else would have',

where the possibilities invoked are metaphysical, just like those that modal chances are supposed to measure. This semantics says that (2.2) will be true if and only if, in the possible world where Oswald does *not* kill Kennedy that is otherwise most like ours, someone else *does* kill Kennedy. Similarly, it says that the conditional

(4.1) 'If coin toss a had been endlessly repeated the limiting frequency of heads would have been p'

will be true if and only if, in the possible world w where a *is* endlessly repeated but is otherwise most like ours, the limiting frequency of heads is p.

The trouble with this view of (4.1) is that, as we noted in chapter 3.II, it assumes an answer to the question of *which* tosses in world w count as 'repeats' of a, i.e. of what the relevant reference class is. The answer, on the modal view, is that the reference class is of coin tosses with the *same possibility* of landing heads that a has. But this is not an answer that possible world semantics can give, since the whole point of – and supposed need for – such semantics lies in denying that metaphysical possibilities are intrinsic features of single worlds.

Modal chances must therefore be rejected not only by those who reject metaphysical possibilities altogether, but also by those who think that, because mere possibilities cannot be intrinsic features of the actual world, only a possible world semantics can make sense of them. This makes it worth looking for something that will do what modal chances do but at a lower metaphysical cost. That means looking for *non*-modal single-case chances which can fix the values of hypothetical limiting frequencies like $f_\infty(Ag)$, $f_\infty(Bg)$ and $f_\infty(Cg)$. And there are such chances: they are called *propensities*.

II

Propensities

If the chances postulated by a *propensity view* of chance do not measure meta-physical possibilities, they cannot be *modal* chances. Nor, if they are single-case chances, can they be frequencies. What then are they?

The short answer is that they are *tendencies*, or *probabilistic dispositions*. The analogy here is with dispositions like *fragility*, which for our purposes may be defined as a disposition to break when subjected to a suitably strong and sudden stress ('suitably' since fragility, like many other dispositions, comes by degrees) or, as I shall say for brevity, when *s-stressed*, e.g. by being dropped a few feet on to a concrete floor. Then the idea is that just as fragility disposes fragile things *always* to break when s-stressed, so a coin toss's chance $CH(H)$ of landing heads disposes tosses with this $CH(H)$ *sometimes* to land heads, i.e. to *tend* to land heads, where $CH(H)$ measures the strength of that tendency.

This answer, however, is ambiguous. There are two dispositions here, both of which have been called propensities by some philosophers, but only one of which can be identified with a coin's chance of landing heads. An example of the one that cannot be so identified is a coin's *bias*, understood as its disposition to have unequal chances of landing heads and tails when tossed. So understood, the bias of a coin is indeed like fragility – the disposition of things to break when s-stressed – but it no more tells us what chances are than fragility tells us what breaking is. On the contrary: for just as we must know what breaking is in order to understand fragility, so we must know what chances are to understand what it is for a coin to be, in this sense, biased. And as with the biases of coins, so with similar probabilistic dispositions, like those altered by flu vaccines which lower our chances of catching flu when exposed to it.

Note, however, that it is not our use of chance to define probabilistic dispositions which stops those dispositions *being* chances: definitions are often used to assert identities. To take a stock example, defining bachelors as un-married males does tell us what bachelors are. Our definitions of dispositions, however, do not tell us what they are, because those definitions are *conditional*: to be fragile is to break *if* s-stressed; for a coin to be biased is for it to have unequal chances of landing heads and tails *if* tossed; and so on. This means that a glass (say) can be fragile when it is not breaking, because it is not then being dropped or otherwise s-stressed, which is why being fragile and breaking are not the same thing.

Similarly with the bias of a coin. Coins can be biased even when they have zero (and thus *equal*) chances of landing heads and tails, because something stops them being tossed. More generally, since a coin's bias entails nothing about its chance of being tossed, it entails nothing about its chance of landing heads. Similarly with the reduced chance that flu vaccines give me of catching flu if exposed to it: this entails nothing about my actual chance of catching flu, since it entails nothing about my chance of being exposed to it. This is why dispositions to have chances cannot *be* – as opposed to being defined by – those chances.

The lack of identity between these dispositions and their defining chances is even clearer when, as in many cases, they are properties of quite different things. The biases of coins, for example, are properties of those coins, which they have whether or not they are being – or are ever – tossed. Chances of landing heads or tails, on the other hand, are properties not of coins but of coin tosses, either of actual or hypothetical classes of them (on frequency views) or of single tosses (on modal or propensity views). That is why, in this book, I ascribe chances of landing heads to coin tosses rather than to coins. And it is why, for a disposition to *be* a chance of landing heads, that disposition must be one which coin tosses can have. What can such a disposition be?

The answer is that it can be a disposition to produce a *limiting frequency* in the sense of chapter 3.v. And that, on what I am here calling the propensity view, is just what single-case chances are. On this view, for a coin toss to have a chance $CH(H) = p$ of landing heads is for it to be such that, *if* there were an endless sequence of tosses with a $CH(H)=p$, that sequence would have a limiting frequency of heads, $f_\infty(H)$, whose value would also be p.

There is indeed a disanalogy, between this and dispositions like fragility, which may seem to make 'disposition' a bad term for propensities so understood. For while the fragility of an object *a* disposes *that very object* to break if s-stressed, a coin toss's propensity to land heads does not dispose *that very toss* to have a limiting frequency of heads. But while this is true, it misses the main point of calling fragility a disposition. The main point is to define fragility not by what *actually* happens to *one* fragile object but by what *would* happen to *any* fragile object if a specified condition were met. Similarly with a coin toss's propensity to land heads, the difference being that the specified condition, and what would happen if it were met, is a condition not on any *one* toss with a chance of landing heads, but on a sequence of such tosses, namely that it be endless. That is what makes it sound odd to call this propensity a disposition of a single coin toss; but what makes it reasonable to do so is the fact that the propensity *is* ascribed to a single toss, whether or not the condition that defines the propensity is met, just as fragility is ascribed to a single object whether or not the condition that defines fragility is met.

This brings us to another objection to this propensity view of chance, namely that whereas most if not all fragile things can be s-stressed, a sequence of coin tosses probably could not be endless, and therefore that the limiting frequency $f_\infty(H)$ could probably not be actual. This, however, really does not matter, as no credible theory of dispositions can, for example, require fragile glasses to break, or even to be able to break: careful furniture removers who make it impossible to s-stress valuable but fragile glasses in transit do not thereby stop them being fragile.

This is not to say that propensities cannot produce actual limiting frequencies, such as those of radium atoms decaying discussed in chapter 3.v. But the fact that they need not do so – just as fragile things need not actually break – makes them dispositions to produce limiting frequencies that need only be *hypothetical* in the sense of chapter 3.VI. However, what this entails depends on what dispositions are, and that, as we shall see in section III, is a contentious issue. But before tackling it, I must make one more point about the special case of propensities: namely, that they are not as special as my having called them tendencies may seem to imply.

The propensity view as stated here does not in fact make propensities differ in kind from dispositions like fragility. For just as fragility disposes *all* fragile things to break if s-stressed, so this propensity view takes having a chance p of landing heads to dispose *all* tosses with that chance to produce a limiting frequency p of heads in an endless sequence of such tosses. That makes both dispositions what I shall call '100%' dispositions, as opposed to mere tendencies, even though I said earlier that tendencies are what propensities are.

But a propensity view need not deny that a coin toss's chance of landing heads *is* a tendency to land heads: it simply identifies that tendency with a 100% disposition to produce a limiting frequency of heads. By so doing it does not make a 0.5 chance of landing heads, say, differ from dispositions like fragility by being a merely 50% disposition to land heads (whatever that might mean). It makes chances differ from other dispositions not in their strength but only in what they are 100% dispositions to produce, namely limiting frequencies. This is why we may expect views of 100% dispositions generally to apply to the special case of propensities.

III

Dispositions

There are two main views of what 100% dispositions are. On the so-called anti-realist view, to be fragile, for example, is simply to break if s-stressed. So while two objects, a fragile and b not, will differ when both are s-stressed, since only a will then break, when they are not s-stressed they need not differ at all, and therefore in particular not by a's having a property of fragility which b lacks.

Whatever its merits, this view of dispositions is useless as a reading of the propensity view that a coin toss's chance $\mathrm{CH}(\mathrm{H})$ of landing heads is a disposition to produce a limiting frequency $f_\infty(\mathrm{H})$. For on an anti-realist view, all this says is that an endless sequence of such tosses *would* have such an $f_\infty(\mathrm{H})$, which is just what the hypothetical limiting frequency view says. If a propensity view is to say more than this, propensities must be more than anti-realist dispositions.

And so, on a realist view of dispositions, they are. This view takes fragile and non-fragile things to differ, even when they are not s-stressed, in a so-called *categorical basis*. That basis may be a property of whatever has the disposition, or some positive or negative combination of such properties and/or of those of its parts: such as the molecular structure which distinguishes glass that is fragile from glass that is not. (Whether only intrinsic properties of things and their parts can figure in the categorical bases of their dispositions is a moot point, although partly terminological, depending – for example – on whether we say that packing a fragile object in bubble-wrap stops it being fragile or stops it being s-stressed. Since for present purposes it does not matter which we say, we may leave the question open.)

Because a realist view of dispositions is needed to distinguish the propensity view of chance from a frequency view, it is the only view of dispositions I shall now consider. I should therefore give at least one argument for it, partly for its own sake but mainly because the argument I shall give also tells us how, and in what sense, propensities can be single-case chances. It does this by showing how realism about dispositions can, oddly enough, meet a common objection to the anti-realist's conditional definition of dispositions. The objection, for example to defining '… is fragile' as '… would break if s-stressed', is that an object a may be fragile even if it would *not* break if s-stressed, because s-stressing a would toughen it and thereby stop it being fragile. And as situations like this, in which a disposition is sometimes said to be *finkish*, may arise for any disposition, the anti-realist definition is always open to such counter-examples.

Realists, on the other hand, can cope with situations that make dispositions finkish by defining '… is fragile' as

'… is F for some F such that … would break if s-stressed *and F'*,

where F is a categorical basis for fragility; and similarly in other cases. Now the basis F may, as we have seen, be a combination of intrinsic properties, positive or negative; so in particular, it may simply be the *absence* of any positive basis for toughness, i.e. for the disposition to *not* break if s-stressed. But even if F is negative in this sense, it will still stop our realist definition of fragility being falsified by finkishness. For on this definition, if s-stressing an object a fails to break it by causing it *not* to be F, if only by giving it a positive basis for toughness, it will also thereby cause it not to be fragile. This is what enables realists to admit, as anti-realists cannot, that objects can be fragile even in situations which make their fragility finkish.

I take this to be a strong argument for realism about dispositions. It may, however, be objected that it assumes a realism about intrinsic properties which *nominalists*, say, who think that only *particulars* exist, will reject. Now while we cannot here consider all the pros and cons of nominalism, we can bypass them, since realists about dispositions can in fact be nominalists. All they need deny is that all factual predicates, however artificial (like the variant of Goodman's '… is grue' which before 2050 (say) applies to things that are *green* and later to things that are *blue*) correspond to *natural* properties. These – which are what from now on I shall mean by 'properties' – may be defined in various ways: for example as those that occur in laws of nature, or those that give things or events which share them similar causal powers.

These and other proposed definitions of natural properties are also debatable, but those debates too we can avoid, provided *some* distinction between natural and other properties (like being grue) is granted. If it is, then for present purposes it is immaterial what natural properties are. They may be *universals*, sets of exactly resembling *tropes* or (as nominalists assert) of actual or possible resembling *particulars*, or something else again. What those alternatives are, and which if any of them is right, are questions we need not ask let alone answer. For all that matters here is that, for example, a fragile *a* and a non-fragile *b* must differ in *some* natural property even when neither is s-stressed. That, as we have seen, is what anti-realists about dispositions deny, and it is all that I shall take realism about dispositions to assert. For this is enough, if chances are indeed dispositions, to make them single-case chances: since it requires two tosses with different chances of landing heads to differ in at least one natural property, in order to provide a categorical basis for the difference in their chances of landing heads.

Nevertheless, just as what I am calling realism about dispositions fails to entail realism about universals, it also, in another sense, fails to entail realism about dispositions themselves. Most realists about fragility, for example, deny that fragility itself is a natural property. They can do this because their realist definition of it only requires an object *a*'s fragility to have a categorical basis *F* such that *a* would break if it were both s-stressed and *F*. It does not require all fragile things to share the *same* basis *F*, and they do not. The molecular structure that makes glass fragile undoubtedly differs from the structure that makes china fragile, and so on. It is variations like this in the categorical bases of dispositions which stop us identifying them with any one of their bases, and these variations also make many realists deny that *any* dispositions are themselves categorical properties.

This assumed dichotomy between dispositions and categorical properties is evident, for example, in the use of realism about dispositions to defend a physicalist philosophy of mind. The view that many mental states, such as beliefs, are dispositions, which anti-realists use to explain those states away, realists use to infer that all mental dispositions have categorical bases, such as more or less complex brain states, that in themselves need be neither mental nor dispositional.

These further claims about categorical properties – that they are all physical and that none of them are dispositions – although often made, remain debatable. But those debates too need not concern us. For all a propensity view of chance needs, in order to distinguish it from the hypothetical limiting frequency view, is the basic realist claim that if any particular thing or event *a* has a disposition *D* which another thing or event *b* lacks, then *a* and *b* must differ in *some* categorical property. Whether *D*'s categorical basis must be physical, and whether it is ever a single property shared by all *D*-things, with which *D* could then be identified, are further questions, which we need not pursue.

IV

Dispositional Chances

To see in more detail how the realist view of dispositions just outlined applies to chances, let us now revisit the law of radioactive decay discussed in chapter 3.III. We saw there that frequentists have to state this law in the form

(3.4) $f_t(D_t x/Rx) = p_t$,

where R is being a radium atom, D_t is decaying within t years and $f_t(D_t x/Rx)$ is the frequency – actual, limiting or hypothetical – among R-atoms of those that do decay within t years. The reason frequentists have to state the law in this form, rather than in the instance

(3.2) $\forall x(Rx \to \text{CH}(D_t x) = p_t)$,

of the universal form

(3.1) $\forall x(Fx \to Gx)$,

normally used to state laws, is – as we noted – that (3.2) credits all R-atoms with single-case chances of which frequency views can make no sense.

Our propensity view, on the other hand, makes easy sense of (3.2), as follows. First, it identifies an R-atom a's having a chance p_t of decaying within t years with a's having some categorical basis (such as a nuclear structure) for a disposition to produce a hypothetical limiting frequency p_t of similar R-atoms decaying within t years. Now while this basis could vary with t, it need not, and in fact does not, do so. Compare Newtonian mechanics, in which a single property – a's inertial mass M – is the categorical basis of all a's myriad dispositions to accelerate under different net forces. In the same way, the theory of radioactivity postulates a single basis for all a's myriad chances of decaying within different time intervals. For just as a's acceleration A under any net force F is given by

(4.2) $A = F/M$,

where M is a constant for all values of F, so the chance p_t is given by

(4.3) $p_t = 1 - e^{-\lambda t}$,

where λ is a constant – radium's so-called *decay constant* – for all values of t. The constant in (4.3) may also be given as radium's *half life* ($= \ln 2/\lambda$), the value of t for which, as we noted in chapter 1.II, $p_t = 1/2$. But however this constant is given, it picks out the same basis for all a's chances of decay, just as the mass M in (4.2) picks out the same basis for all a's dispositions to accelerate.

This analogy between λ and M is, however, limited. For while all dispositions to accelerate will have the same basis – an inertial mass – in equally massive objects of all kinds, a given set of propensities to decay could have different bases (different nuclear structures) in different radioelements; just as we noted in section III that fragility has different bases in glass and china. That is, a quite different nuclear structure in a different radioelement S could make S share radium's instability by making S-atoms satisfy (4.3) for the same value of λ. This means that λ, unlike M, may no more have a single basis than fragility does.

Suppose however that, at least in radium, there *is* a single basis L for λ and hence, for all t, for the chance $\text{CH}(D_t) = p_t$ of any one R-atom decaying within t years. It follows on the propensity view of chance that, for all t,

$f_{\infty t}(D_t x/Rx \wedge Lx) = p_t$,

where $f_{\infty t}(D_t x / Rx \wedge Lx)$ is the hypothetical limiting frequency, among R-atoms that are L, of those that decay within t years. But as by hypothesis all R-atoms *are* L, it also follows for all t that

$$f_{\infty t}(D_t x / Rx) = p_t,$$

which is the hypothetical limiting frequency version of (3.4). This shows how the law of radium's decay can both have the form (3.2) of a universal generalisation and entail a relative frequency of the form (3.4).

The same goes for all probabilistic laws. The propensity view lets all of them be stated as universal generalisations of the form (in simple cases)

$$\forall x(Fx \rightarrow Lx),$$

where L is a basis of a propensity to yield a hypothetical limiting frequency p of F-things that are G, for some G. This is how the propensity view can dispense with the distinction which we saw in chapter 3.III that frequentists must draw between the forms

(3.1) $\forall x(Fx \rightarrow Gx)$ and
(3.3) $f(Gx / Fx) = p$

of deterministic and probabilistic laws linking F and G. On the propensity view, all instances of (3.3) which express laws will follow from instances of (3.1).

So much for the chances that occur in laws. What of chances which seem *not* to occur in laws, like those of coin tosses landing heads? Do these chances also have a categorical basis in properties of individual coin tosses, as the propensity view says? There are really two questions here. The first is whether these chances exist at all, a question to which we shall return in section VII when we have finished looking at different views of what chances are. The second question is whether, assuming that chances of coin tosses landing heads do exist, in some sense which links them to how often coin tosses *do* land heads, we must credit *single* tosses with chances of landing heads. This is the question that concerns us here: are there single-case chances of coin tosses landing heads?

One common reason for denying that there are rests on the common if contentious claim that single-case chances other than 1 and 0 are inconsistent with *determinism*, which for present purposes we may take to say that the future is fixed by the present. This may be no objection to the propensity view of radioactivity, where determinism is generally thought to be made false by the absence of so-called *hidden variables*. That is, radium atoms which *will* decay before any given future time do not differ now in *any* natural property from atoms that will *not* decay before that time. In other words, neither the future state nor the future existence of these atoms is fixed by anything in the present.

But even if determinism is false of radioactivity, it may still be true of how coin tosses land; and most people think it is. That is, they think that two present coin tosses a and b, where a will land heads and b will not, must differ in some present respect that fixes which way each toss will land. If that is so, how can a and b also have single-case chances, between 1 and 0, of landing heads? If they cannot, then the chances of coin tosses landing heads must be frequencies, not propensities.

A propensity view of these chances may be defended against this argument in one of two ways. One way is to put coin tosses on a par with radium atoms by denying that their relevant futures are determined by present hidden variables. This is not to deny that two tosses like *a* and *b* will differ in *some* ways before they land – they almost certainly will – merely that any such difference will make them land differently.

The other way to defend a propensity view of these chances is to say that, even if the outcomes of coin tosses are fixed in advance, this need not stop them also having single-case chances other than 1 or 0. For on the propensity view, all this means is that these tosses have *some* property (or combination of properties) F such that an endless sequence of F-tosses would have a limiting frequency $f_\infty(H)$ between 1 and 0. And this is quite compatible with some F-tosses having another property or combination of properties G such that all and only F-tosses which are also G will in fact land heads.

However, these two responses only show how, in a relevantly deterministic world, single coin tosses *could* have chances other than 0 or 1 of landing heads. Neither response gives a positive reason to think that they do have such chances. One reason to think that they do may be put as a dilemma for determinists, by asking what it means to say in our example that a coin toss being F and G *determines* it to land heads. For on the one hand, on the Humean reading of chapter 3.III, all this means is that all coin tosses that are both F and G *do* land heads, which is compatible with a lower frequency – actual, limiting or hypothetical – of F-tosses in general landing heads.

On the other hand, a non-Humean reading of determinism will have to credit each toss that is both F and G with a single-case chance $\text{CH}(H) = 1$ of landing heads. But that makes the conjunction $F \wedge G$ the categorical basis of a deterministic propensity, a disposition of all $F \wedge G$-tosses to produce, not just an actual $f(H)=1$, but a hypothetical limiting $f_\infty(H)=1$. But no one who accepts *this* propensity can rule out *all* propensities. And a special argument will then be needed to show why this deterministic propensity prevents F disposing all F-tosses to produce a lower hypothetical limiting frequency of heads; and I know of no such argument.

Still, even if this dilemma faces determinists with the same choice between frequencies and propensities that others face, it need not make anyone choose the latter. An argument for choosing propensities does arise, however, if we press a question we first asked in chapter 3.III: namely, *which* frequencies are chances? We said there that a Humean test for when statistical correlations are statistical laws might answer that question. But it will only do so for chances, like those of radioactive decay, which occur in laws. It is less obvious how Humean criteria for laws apply to chances that may not occur in laws, like those of coin tosses landing heads. The propensity view, on the other hand, offers an immediate answer in all these cases to the question of whether a frequency is, or at least corresponds to, a chance, as follows.

In chapter 3.VI, we asked what fixes the value of a hypothetical limiting frequency $f_\infty(H)$ of coin tosses landing heads. But we did not then ask *which* coin tosses have this limiting frequency. This is the question which was raised for possible-world semantics at the end of section I, and which is just as hard for frequentists to answer when the coin tosses, and hence the frequency of heads, are hypothetical.

On the propensity view the answer to this question is as simple as we saw in section I that it is on the modal view. For on the propensity view, as we have seen, a coin toss a's chance $\mathrm{CH}(H)$ of landing heads is a disposition whose basis F is a property or combination of properties which a actually has. So the answer to our question is just this: the hypothetical tosses that have the hypothetical $f_\infty(H)$ which $\mathrm{CH}(H)$ disposes a to produce are F-tosses; and similarly in all other cases.

But how, it may be asked, can we identify the categorical bases of chances, and how can we measure the merely hypothetical limiting frequencies that give those chances their value? Those questions, however, serious though they are, are for scientific theory and observation to answer, not for us. All that concerns us here is that those questions *have* answers, a fact of which the propensity view makes more apparent sense than frequency views do.

The propensity view does, however, face two objections to which frequency views are immune and which we should therefore consider here. One is that the view does not entail, and so cannot explain, the rules of numerical probability we stated again in chapter 3.IV, such as:

(1.4)   All probabilities lie between 0 and 1 inclusive, i.e.
$$0 \le \mathrm{P}(A) \le 1;$$

(1.5)   The probabilities of A and ¬A always add up to 1, i.e.
$$\mathrm{P}(A) + \mathrm{P}(\neg A) = 1.$$

The reason the propensity view fails to make chances satisfy (1.4) and (1.5) is that it only requires chances to *correspond* to hypothetical limiting frequencies, which they could do without sharing their values. (They could for example be twice the frequencies they correspond to, thus making their own values range from 0 to 2.)

However, although propensities *need* not satisfy (1.4) and (1.5), we do have a reason to make them do so. The reason is that here, as elsewhere, it is convenient to measure a quantity by its effects. That for example is how we measure another quantitative disposition, solubility: by the amount S of solute that will dissolve in a litre (say) of solvent. Here too we could use another measure, such as $2 \times S$, or any other function $g(S)$ that is strongly order-preserving, i.e. such that $g(S') > g(S)$ if $S' > S$. The reason we use S itself is that S is the simplest measure of solubility.

Similarly with propensities, and indeed with the modal chances of section I. On both views of chance we measure $\mathrm{CH}(H)$ by the $f_\infty(H)$ it entails, not because we could not use suitable functions of $f_\infty(H)$, but because it is simpler to use $f_\infty(H)$ itself. And once we do so, that makes propensities and modal chances satisfy these rules of numerical probability, simply because frequencies do.

The second objection to propensities that we need to consider is a charge of vacuous circularity. The alleged circularity lies in postulating a single-case disposition $\mathrm{CH}(H)$ to yield a hypothetical limiting frequency $f_\infty(H)$ that serves only to measure the very disposition which, by definition, entails it. For as neither $\mathrm{CH}(H)$ nor $f_\infty(H)$ can be directly observed, postulating them looks like bootstrapping: that is, using two otherwise unsupported hypotheses to provide specious support for each other. What independent reason do we ever have to believe either in actual propensities or in the hypothetical limiting frequencies which they are dispositions to produce?

The answer to this rhetorical question lies in our reasons for postulating laws containing chances, such as those in microphysics, genetics and elsewhere that we cited in chapter 1.II. We do so because we think that many of the *actual* frequencies we observe need explaining: that they are not just brute facts. When and why we should think this are questions I shall return to later, when we see what makes observed frequencies evidence for chances. Here it must suffice that their being evidence for chances can also make them evidence for hypothetical limiting frequencies and hence, arguably, for dispositions with bases, i.e. for propensities, which can then explain the actual frequencies we observe.

V

Chance and Necessity

This almost completes the task set at the end of section I, to find non-modal substitutes for modal chances. The substitutes are propensities, which can as we have seen be single-case chances, just as modal chances can. They are also non-modal in the relevant sense, since their bases are simply combinations of natural properties. For while propensities do postulate possibilities – such as the possible members of hypothetical infinite classes with limiting frequencies – these are no more problematic than other possibilities which everyone must admit.

Suppose for example we think the universe could be slightly larger than it is. To think this is to postulate merely possible spacetime regions with infinities of merely possible spacetime points. Whatever sense we make of these, say by a possible-world semantics of the kind sketched again in section I, we can, as we saw there, make exactly the same sense of the infinity of merely possible coin tosses which an actual toss's propensity to land heads involves.

What propensities do *not* involve are the problematic possibilities that modal chances measure, of which we saw in section I that no possible-world semantics can make sense, because these possibilities need to be features of single worlds. These are the possibilities for which propensities provide non-modal substitutes, in the non-modal bases that determine, for example, which hypothetical coin tosses are in the reference class with the limiting frequency that a propensity to land heads entails: namely, tosses which share that propensity's non-modal basis.

What then of the possibilities postulated by the ergodic hypothesis of section I? Are those possibilities, for example of the gas system g being in the states A, B and C listed in Table 1, as innocuous as the possibilities of non-actual spacetime points and merely hypothetical coin tosses? If they are not, then rejecting modal chances may mean rejecting an important if controversial scientific hypothesis.

But if they are, we should be able to give a credible propensity reading of that hypothesis. How may we do that?

First, the propensity view can certainly admit that, for the gas sample g to have non-zero chances, CH(Ag), CH(Bg) and CH(Cg), of being in the states A, B and C at any one time, it must be *possible* for g to *be* in each of those states at that time. For in themselves these possibilities are as innocent as those of g having temperatures other than the temperature T that it actually has. So these possibilities are not the issue. The issue is whether the ergodic hypothesis requires the three chances CH(Ag), CH(Bg) and CH(Cg) to measure *how* possible it is for g to be A, B and C respectively. And the fact is that it does not require this, even though it says that if g 'stayed long enough in any one macrostate T it would be

(i)   in each possible microstate compatible with T at some time, and
(ii) in any given set of those states for a length of time proportional to a probability measure of that set.'

For in order for (ii) to be true, the probability measures of the states Ag, Bg and Cg need only be the hypothetical limiting frequencies, as defined in section I, of the time g spends in those states, or the dispositions which g has at any one time to have those limiting frequencies.

So far so good for our non-modal substitutes for modal chances. But there is a snag. Because propensities are metaphysically cheaper than modal chances, they do not entail a thesis which modal chances do entail and which I have so far taken for granted. This thesis – which for reasons that will become clear shortly I shall call the *necessity thesis* (NT) – says that for any proposition A,

(NT) CH(A)=1 $\Rightarrow$ A, or, since P(A)=1−P(¬A), CH(A)=0 $\Rightarrow$ ¬A.

Note that (NT) is only tenable as a thesis about *chance*, not as a thesis about any other kind of probability. Its epistemic counterpart is false for the same reason that a proposition A entailed by a proposition B may be false: namely, that B may be false. For this same possibility, of B's falsehood, also lets A be false even if EP(A|B), A's epistemic probability given B, is 1. And (NT)'s counterpart for credences is false for an even simpler reason: namely, that, with a few Cartesian and debatable perceptual exceptions ('I think', 'I exist', 'I am seeing something red' ...), believing A, however strongly, never entails that A is true.

For chances, however, (NT) is very plausible, and I have tacitly assumed it throughout my discussions of chance. In particular, I assumed it in chapter 3.III in conjecturing that sufficient causes 'necessitate their effects by giving them no – i.e. zero – chance of not occurring'. For while something which does not happen may still be necessary in some senses – it may for example be morally necessary – it cannot be necessary in any factual sense. This being so, sufficient causes can only make their effects necessary by giving them zero chances of not occurring if (NT) is true. Yet, as we shall now see, (NT) is not easily reconciled with limiting frequency or propensity views of chance.

I said in 3.III that frequentism lets those whom I there called Humeans agree, for example, that tossing a coin can necessitate its *landing*, if not its landing heads. For on any frequency view the fact that 'in the relevant circumstances . . . tossed coin *always* land' makes their Humean chance of landing 1 and hence their Humean chance of not landing 0. It also satisfies (NT), since if a proposition L says, of any actual coin toss, that it lands, then the fact that *all* actual tosses land entails, as (NT) requires, that L is true and thus that ¬L is false.

So far so good for what in chapter 3.IV I called frequentism's 'non-modal surrogates' for necessity and possibility, namely:

what is *necessary* → what *always* happens;
what is *impossible* → what *never* happens;
what is *possible* → what *sometimes* happens.

It is not however good enough for the quantitative surrogate

how possible something is → *how frequently* it happens.

The reason is that some frequencies, including those that propensities entail, fail to satisfy (NT), since they let coin tosses, for example, fail to land even when the frequency of their landing is 1. For frequencies which allow that failure, $f(L) = 1$ does not entail L, and $f(L) = 0$ does not entail ¬L. When and how can this occur?

The answer is that while it cannot occur with *finite* frequencies – since in a finite class of coin tosses, the frequency of those that land can only be 1 if they *all* land – it can happen with *limiting* frequencies, as in the following hypothetical sequence of coin tosses, where for some reason some tosses do not land at all.

Number n of tosses	100	1000	10,000	100,000
Number of landings L	99	991	9,920	99,300
Number of non-landings ¬L	1	9	80	700
Frequency $f_n(L)$ of landings	0.99	0.991	0.992	0.993

This shows how coin tosses could have a limiting frequency 1 of landing even if infinitely many of them do *not* land. This means that hypothetical limiting frequencies cannot satisfy (NT). Nor therefore can propensities, since they are dispositions to produce hypothetical limiting frequencies. A coin toss may fail to land even if its propensity to land is 1.

Should this make us reject propensities or reject (NT)? The case for rejecting (NT) is that it faces serious counter-examples, one of them the spinning pointer P of chapter 2. For suppose P does in fact have an equal chance $n/360$ of stopping in any $n°$ angle, as it may well do. On this density distribution of chances, as on any other continuous distribution, P's chance of stopping at any one *point* will be zero. Yet since P must stop at *some* point, it must be possible for it to stop there, despite having a zero chance of doing so. But then (NT) must be false.

This and other counter-examples to (NT) can be rebutted, for example by crediting P with an infinitesimal chance of stopping at a point, or by denying that it can stop at one point without also stopping at neighbouring ones. But these rebuttals are neither natural nor easy to make good. So why bother to keep a thesis with so many counter-examples which is not entailed by either the hypothetical limiting frequency or the propensity views of chance?

There are two reasons for wanting to keep (NT). One is a desire to save the intuition that nothing can happen which has a zero chance of happening. The other is the fact that, by failing to satisfy (NT), the propensity view creates an unfortunate gap between deterministic and probabilistic laws. For while the view can, as we noted in section IV, give laws of both kinds the universal form

(3.1) $\forall x(Fx \rightarrow Gx)$,

which no frequency view can do, only if (NT) is true will (3.1) follow from

$\forall x(Fx \rightarrow \text{CH}(Gx)=1)$,

as it arguably should. For as we have seen, if (NT) is false, the fact that every F-thing has a chance 1 of being G will not entail that *all* F-things are G. How then, for these or other reasons, might we save (NT)?

VI

Modality *versus* Propensity

I think that only the modal view of chance discussed in section I can save (NT), because it is the only tenable view of chance which takes chances to measure possibilities. For it is an uncontentious principle of modal logic, which I shall call (NP), that for any proposition A, and in any sense of necessity and corresponding sense of possibility,

(NP) A is *necessary* if and only if ¬A is *not possible*, so that
A is *possible* if and only if ¬A is *not necessary*, and
A is *impossible* if and only if ¬A is *necessary*.

Given (NP), chances cannot be modal, i.e. measure possibilities, if a proposition A that *is* possible can have the same chance as a proposition B that is not, i.e. is such that ¬B is necessary. Yet as we saw in section V, the possible proposition A that a coin toss does *not* land can share the hypothetical limiting frequency – zero – of the impossible proposition B that the toss both does and does not land.

From this it follows that while modal chances can entail hypothetical limiting frequencies, as in section I they do by definition, the converse entailment cannot hold for limiting frequencies of 1 and 0. Note that this does not rule out the *modality-to-frequency* assumption (MF) of section I, which says that

(MF) If the possibility of any F-thing being G is greater than or equal to that of any F'-thing being G', then $f_\infty(Gx/Fx) \geq f_\infty(G'x/F'x)$.

For all (MF) entails, when it is possible for F-things to be G, but not for F'-things to be G', is that $f_\infty(Gx/Fx) \geq f_\infty(G'x/F'x)$, and this allows both $f_\infty(Gx/Fx)$ and $f_\infty(G'x/F'x)$ to be zero. What is ruled out is identifying modal chances with propensities, i.e. with dispositions to produce hypothetical limiting frequencies, since that would make equal limiting frequencies entail equal chances. So if chances *are* modal, i.e. do measure possibilities, the propensity view cannot be right.

This gives us a clear if unattractive choice between two incompatible views of single-case chances. The metaphysically cheap propensity view can accept all the objections to (NT) but can make no sense of the idea that chances measure metaphysical possibilities. The metaphysically more expensive modal view preserves (NT) by adopting that idea, but must then explain away (NT)'s many plausible counter-examples while postulating metaphysical possibilities of which possible-world semantics make no sense.

Given these alternatives, it is hardly surprising that many philosophers reject single-case chances altogether. But that is no easy option either, as the problems of the frequency views discussed in chapter 3 show. Hence the appeal of an even more radical *subjective* view that rejects *all* chances, offering instead subjective surrogates which only entail credences, i.e. degrees of belief. How, and how well, these surrogates for chances work we shall only be able to see after more has been said about what credences are and how we get them; and that will be done in the next few chapters. But first I shall end this chapter by asking what it *means* to deny that chances exist, a denial whose content the variety of views of chance we have been discussing makes less obvious at first sight than it needs to be.

VII

The Existence of Chances

In chapter 1.I, in distinguishing three kinds of probability, I required chances to be objective by characterising them as follows:

> *Chances* are real features of the world. They show up, in [our] examples, in how often people get cancer and coin tosses land heads, and they are affected by whether people smoke and by how coins are tossed. Chances are what they are whether or not we ever conceive of or know about them, and so they are neither relative to evidence nor mere matters of opinion, with no opinion any better than any other.

As all the views of chance so far discussed fit this objective bill, we might expect subjectivists to deny the existence of chances as defined by any of those views. But they cannot do that, since they cannot reject *actual finite frequencies*, such as the fractions of people who get cancer in any given year. No one can deny that these fractions exist and satisfy both the rules of numerical probability and the above description of objective chances. So to make the existence of objective chance a serious question, we must take 'chance' to mean something more than actual finite frequencies, which from now on, when I need to make this point, I shall call *statistical probabilities* rather than chances.

What then should subjectivists reject, if not actual finite frequencies? Should they, for example, reject *limiting* frequencies in actually infinite classes, like those discussed in chapter 3.V of radium atoms decaying within various time intervals? Arguably not: for why deny that actual finite frequencies can have actual limits?

Take the class of all people, past, present and future. This, because it includes *all* people, is what in 3.v I called a *maximal* reference class, noting that statisticians normally identify probabilities only with frequencies in such classes. But if the human race goes on for ever, as it conceivably might, this class will be infinite. If it is, then the statistical probability of members of the race as a whole getting cancer (say) cannot be any actual finite frequency. So the only way to stop this probability entailing our eventual extinction is to let statistical probabilities be, if necessary, limiting frequencies, and to accept that such frequencies can, if actual, exist. For this reason, which I admit is not conclusive, I am inclined to think that would-be subjectivists about chance, because they cannot reject actual finite frequencies, should also accept actual limiting frequencies, counting them as mere statistical probabilities rather than chances.

Hypothetical limiting frequencies are another matter entirely, for even if a reference class is actually infinite, any limiting frequency in it might be changed by adding a further infinity of merely possible members. Subjectivists who accept actual limiting frequencies may therefore consistently reject hypothetical ones, and I shall assume that they do. They cannot, however, do so just because hypothetical frequencies are not *actual*, for they do not claim to be actual. As noted in section III, a hypothetical frequency is like the hypothetical breaking of a fragile glass *a* that is not actually under stress. For what was there called the anti-realist view, that *a* need not *actually* differ from an unstressed glass *b* which is *not* fragile, still takes *a* to be fragile and *b* not. It simply makes this a difference between two non-actual situations: one in which *a* is s-stressed and breaks and the other in which *b* is s-stressed and does not break.

Similarly, on the analogous hypothetical limiting frequency view of chance, while coin tosses *a* and *b*, with different chances of landing heads, need not *actually* differ, *a* and *b* will still differ hypothetically, in the different limiting frequencies of heads that *would* result if they were endlessly repeated. This therefore is what I shall take subjectivists about chance to deny of *any* toss: that if it were endlessly repeated, there would be *any* limiting frequency of heads; and similarly for all other alleged hypothetical limiting frequencies (other than 1 or 0, produced by deterministic dispositions like fragility).

And if there are no hypothetical limiting frequencies other than 1 and 0, there will also be no dispositions to produce them, and hence no single-case chances other than 1 and 0. For the only views that we have seen to make sense of single-case chances take them either to *be* dispositions to produce hypothetical limiting frequencies (the propensity view) or to entail such dispositions (the modal view). These too I shall therefore take subjectivists about chance to reject.

This means that what seem to me the three best candidates for *being* chances – modal chances, propensities and hypothetical limiting frequencies – are the very three whose existence I think subjectivists about chance can and should deny. This being so, I shall assume from now on that objective chances are one or other of these three, and therefore that they either are or entail the last and least of them, namely hypothetical limiting frequencies. Whether they are anything more than that, and if so what more, are questions which, having set out the pros and cons in this and earlier chapters, I shall leave readers to decide.

Further Reading

The classic source of the propensity view of chance is Popper, in his (1957), reprinted in Miller (1983), and his (1990), pp. 9–12. A variant of the view is more fully worked out in my (1971), especially chapters 1–4, and the view is discussed in its historical context in chapters 6–7 of Gillies (2000). A substantial introductory overview of chance as it features in physics, including a discussion of the ergodic hypothesis, is given in chapter 3 of Sklar (1992).

For possibility, Loux's (1979) contains good articles on the metaphysics of modality, especially Lewis (1973c), Adams (1974), Stalnaker (1976), and Plantinga (1976). For more details of Lewis's possible-world semantics, see his (1973b).

For an anti-realist view of dispositions, see chapter 5 of Ryle (1949); for a realist view, see chapter 6.6 of Armstrong (1993). For a later and more detailed realist view of dispositions see Mumford (1998), and for an opinionated survey of views of the semantics and ontology of dispositions, see my (2000b).

For 'grue', see Goodman (1965); for properties, see the papers in Mellor and Oliver (1997), especially Lewis (1983), Shoemaker (1980) and my (1997).

For apparent counter-examples to the (NT) principle that $\text{CH}(A)=1 \Rightarrow A$, and defences against them, see my (2000a).

5
Credence

I

Degrees of Belief

Some reasons for taking belief to come by degrees were sketched in chapter 1.IV. One was that we can *doubt* any contingent proposition A, which cannot just mean that we do not believe A, for that will be true if we have never thought of A. Nor can doubting A mean *disbelieving* A, i.e. believing its negation ¬A, since we can doubt both A and ¬A at once. Doubt must therefore be a so-called *propositional attitude* in its own right; or rather, since it comes by degrees, it must be a family of attitudes, ranging from near-belief to near-disbelief.

The simplest explanation of this fact is that belief also comes by degrees, ranging from full belief in A to full disbelief in A, i.e. to full belief in its negation, ¬A. If it does, we can relate doubt to belief in either of two ways, depending on how we think of it. If we think of doubt as uncertainty *that* A, we can equate degrees of doubt in A with degrees of belief in ¬A. If we think of it as uncertainty about *whether* A, we can measure it by how close our degrees of belief in A and in ¬A are to each other. Which way is the better does not matter here, since either way we can hardly have degrees of doubt without degrees of belief.

Still, none of this shows that degrees of belief have a *probability* measure, since it does not show that belief comes by *quantitative* degrees. By this I mean that we could believe one proposition more strongly than another without there being any measure of *how much* more strongly we do so. How can we measure that?

We could easily give belief a quantitative measure if we identified believing a proposition A to degree p with believing that A has a chance or an epistemic probability p. That however, as we noted in chapter 1.IV, would make the very idea of degrees of belief redundant, which it is not. For we can certainly say or think that A is more or less probable without crediting A with any chance or evidential probability. I need not, for example, take my willingness to offer odds of 4:1 against Pink Gin winning the Derby to rest on anything more than a hunch. That is, I need not believe that the horse has a low objective chance of winning, nor even, relative to what I know, a low evidential probability of winning. I need only have, for no reason I can think of, a low degree of belief in his winning.

Or take the determinists of chapter 4.IV, who think that a single-case chance of a coin toss *a* landing heads can only be 1 or 0. They may still think, speak and act as if the proposition that *a* will land heads has, in some sense, a probability of 1/2; and they may do so even if they know they have no evidence at all about *a*'s prospects of landing heads. This does not show that they have inconsistent beliefs about *a*, or even that they must be invoking the indifference principle of chapter 2.VI. They may, for no special reason, simply happen to have equal degrees of belief in the contradictory propositions that *a* will land heads and that it will not.

These and other arguments for the view that belief comes by degrees may not be conclusive, but all that matters here is that the view is widely held. This is enough to give probability a psychological application which we need to discuss. That is why, in what follows, we may take it for granted that degrees of belief exist which are not just full beliefs in chances or epistemic probabilities.

Even so, we still need to see what makes degrees of belief quantitative and, in particular, what makes them probabilities. For if degrees of belief are not full beliefs in probabilities of other kinds, we cannot use those probabilities to give degrees of belief a probability measure. Indeed in the case of epistemic probability it is the other way round, as we shall see in chapter 6: epistemic probabilities get their measure from that of belief, whose measure must therefore come from somewhere else.

Where then does belief's probability measure come from? Not from chance, which we saw in chapters 3 and 4 gets its measure from the limiting frequencies which chances entail. For degrees of belief entail neither frequencies nor, given that (as I have just argued) they do not entail beliefs about chances, beliefs about frequencies. If my degree of belief in a coin toss landing heads need not make me believe that it has a corresponding chance of landing heads, it need not make me believe that an endless sequence of similar tosses would have a limiting frequuency of heads. So the fact that such a frequency satisfies the rules of numerical probability cannot be what makes my degree of belief do so.

We cannot therefore get a probability measure of belief from the probability measure of chance. Nor can we get it from the assumption, to be discussed later, that if my only evidence about a proposition A is that it has a chance *p* of being true, then my credence in A should also be *p*. For this assumption *presupposes* a probability measure of belief: it does not provide one. Without such a measure, the most we can assume is that, if my only evidence about A and B is that A's chance is greater than B's, I should believe A more strongly than I believe B. How much more strongly is a question we cannot even ask without a quantitative measure of belief which neither chances nor full beliefs about chances will provide. To find that measure we must look elsewhere; and we start with betting.

II

Betting and Belief

One way of telling how strongly you believe a proposition A, say that Pink Gin will win the Derby, is to offer you a bet on it. Other things being equal, the more strongly you believe A, the shorter the odds at which you will bet that A is true, a fact that we can use to provide a measure of your degree of belief. To show how, we must first explain some betting terms, starting with 'odds'.

Suppose I offer you a bet on A as follows. I ask you to pay N units of some currency (pounds, dollars, euros, yen . . .) and offer to pay M units to make a *stake* of M+N units, which *you* will win if A turns out to be true and *I* will win if it turns out to be false. In other words – which will prove useful when the idea of betting is generalised in section V – I offer you a *benefit* of M+N units if you win at a *cost* to you of N units. To do this is to offer you odds of N:M *on* A or of M:N *against* A. Thus, in the example of chapter 1.I, where you bet me that Pink Gin will win at 4:1 *against*, you risk losing 1 unit in order to gain 4 if you win; betting at 4:1 *on*, you risk losing 4 units in order to gain 1 if you win; and so on. (To bet at *evens* (1:1) is to risk losing 1 unit in order to gain 1 if you win.)

Although the terms of bets are usually given as odds, it will be simpler for us to use so-called *betting quotients*, which are related to odds as follows. For a bet on A, to offer odds of N:M *on*, or M:N *against*, is to offer the quotient N/(M+N). So your quotient for a bet which you will win if A is true is the fraction of the stake that you put up, or what I prefer to call the bet's *cost/benefit* or c/b ratio: i.e. the ratio of what the bet costs you if you lose to the benefit to you if you win.

Then the question whose answer is taken to reflect your degree of belief in A is this: what is the *greatest* quotient or c/b ratio p you would accept for a bet on A if – among other things – you could afford the bet, wanted to win it, and had no other interest in whether A is true? Or, simplifying the question by assuming a unit stake or benefit: what is the greatest value of p for which, on these assumptions, you would risk losing p units if A is false to win 1 unit if A is true?

The significance of an answer to this question must not be misunderstood. It does not *define* degrees of belief any more than thermometer readings define temperatures. We infer temperatures from thermometer readings without taking those readings to define or explain the temperatures we infer from them. It is the other way round: that is, it is temperatures which explain the readings we infer them from, not *vice versa*. Far from defining temperatures, our use of thermometers presupposes both a prior concept of temperature and a theory which tells us how to make thermometers measure temperature and not something else. It tells us for example that if you want a thermometer to measure the outside air temperature on a sunny day, you should read it in the shade, to ensure that it is affected only by the air temperature and not by the sun's radiation.

Similarly with using c/b ratios to measure degrees of belief. In practice, the highest ratio you will accept for a bet on A will be affected not only by your degree of belief in A but by other factors: whether you want to bet at all, what stakes you prefer to bet for, whether you want A or ¬A to be true, and so on. Hence the precautions, such as those listed above, which are meant to stop these other factors affecting p; just as measuring air temperatures in the shade is meant to stop the sun's radiation affecting that measurement.

However, while most experts agree on how to make thermometer readings accurate, there is less agreement on the conditions needed to make your choices of c/b ratios measure your degrees of belief. Fortunately this does not matter, provided we can agree that *some* such conditions exist. For while we use *actual* thermometer readings to measure temperatures, we are not asking you to accept a c/b ratio for an *actual* bet, merely to introspect the strength of your belief in the proposition to be bet on. Betting talk is only designed to help you to do this, and to provide a way of expressing your degree of belief in A: namely, as the greatest c/b ratio p for a bet on A which that degree of belief would make you accept if nothing else affected your choice of p.

The fact that you are only being asked to choose c/b ratios for *hypothetical* bets on propositions has one important consequence that is often overlooked. This is that it does not matter how, or even whether, an actual bet could be settled. Take for example any universal generalisation of the form

(3.1) $\forall x(Fx \to Gx)$

discussed in chapter 3.III. Then, as many philosophers have remarked, while observing instances of (3.1) can *falsify* it, by revealing an F-thing that is not G, it cannot *verify* it: for however many F-things we see to be G, there may always be others, as yet unseen, which are not G. So while a bet on (3.1) that has to be settled by observing its instances can certainly be lost, it can never be won.

From this it may seem to follow that no one should accept *any* non-zero c/b ratio for a bet on (3.1) and hence that our degree of belief in it should be zero. In fact this does not follow, since our question about (3.1) is only hypothetical: what is the greatest c/b ratio you would accept for a bet on (3.1) that *could* be settled either way – perhaps by revelation – so that you would win if (3.1) is true, just as you would lose if (3.1) is false. That c/b ratio need not be zero, and nor therefore need the introspectible degree of belief in (3.1) which it measures.

So far so good for introspection. But its significance must not be exaggerated. It does not make our degrees of belief whatever we think they are. It merely exploits the truism that, on the whole, we know more about what we believe, and about how strongly we believe it, than others do. That truism is part of our so-called *folk psychology*, another part of which the decision theories sketched in chapter 1.IV exploit by extending to degrees of belief and desire the commonplace idea that by and large we do what we believe will get us what we want.

Take for example my belief that the small Cambridgeshire city of Ely has only one really good restaurant. This disposes me, among other things, to go to Ely if I want to dine at that restaurant and to go elsewhere if I want to dine really well at another restaurant. Similarly with degrees of belief: your degree of belief in a proposition A will dispose you, among other things, to accept c/b ratios only up to some value p for bets on A in conditions, like those listed above, which stop other factors affecting the value of p.

Moreover, on the realist view of dispositions outlined in 4.III, a disposition to accept some c/b ratios and not others is one you can have whether you know it or not. The knowledge of our own beliefs which our invitation to introspect them exploits is indeed an important feature of belief, which a complete theory of it needs to explain. But it is not a precondition for *having* degrees of belief which entail dispositions to accept some bets and reject others. And that entailment is all it takes to give degrees of belief a probability measure.

III

Coherence

I shall assume therefore that the greatest c/b ratio p you are disposed, in suitable conditions, to accept for a bet on a proposition A measures your degree of belief in A. It does not yet follow that this measure is a probability, i.e. that it satisfies the rules of numerical probability given in chapter 1. Why for example should this betting measure satisfy

(1.4) All probabilities lie between 0 and 1 inclusive, i.e.
$0 \leq P(A) \leq 1$, or

(1.5) The probabilities of A and of ¬A always add up to 1, i.e.
$P(A) + P(\neg A) = 1$?

To see that our betting measure of belief will in fact satisfy (1.4), we first recall from section II that, by definition, your c/b ratio for a bet which you will win if A is true is the fraction of the stake you put up. We now make the so-called *coherence* assumption that *we will not accept terms, for bets we want to win, that will make us certain to lose whatever happens*. This lets us assume that you will not pay more for a bet than you will get back if you win, and that your opponent will not let you pay less than nothing, i.e. will not pay you to bet. This ensures that, as (1.4) requires, no c/b ratio that you accept will be greater than 1 or less than 0.

Within these limits, we may also assume that the greater your degree of belief in A, the greater p will be, on the grounds that

(5.1) the surer you are *that* A is true, the less you need to gain *if* A is true to make you risk losing your share of the stake if A is false.

Adding this assumption to coherence makes p a measure, of your belief in A, which ranges from $p = 1$ for full belief in A to $p = 0$ for full belief in ¬A.

So much for (1.4): what of (1.5)? Why, if at any one time you will risk losing

(i) p units to win 1 if A is true, and
(ii) q units to win 1 if ¬A is true,

should $p + q = 1$? Here too the answer is standardly taken to lie in the coherence assumption that no parties to bets will accept c/b ratios which make them certain to lose whatever happens. From this assumption several so-called *Dutch Book* arguments have been devised to show that p and q must add up to 1, since only then will you be immune to a Dutch Book, i.e. to a combination of bets (i) and (ii) that *will* make you lose overall whatever happens. One such argument, taken from Jeffrey (1983), chapter 4.2, is laid out in Table 2 below. This table gives your gains on bets (i) and (ii), and your net gain on their combination, if A is true and if A is false; and shows thereby that your net gain will be the same whether A is true or false: positive if $p + q$ is less than 1 and negative if $p + q$ is greater than 1. And while you will not mind certainly winning whatever happens, your opponent will certainly mind certainly losing whatever happens, so that coherence will stop him or her from accepting any such bet and hence you from making it. Only if $p + q = 1$, when your net gain is zero, can both parties bet coherently, i.e. with neither being certain to lose whatever happens. And as in this case, so in all. All coherent c/b ratios satisfy (1.5) as well as (1.4).

Your gains	if A	if ¬A
on bet (i)	$1-p$	$-p$
on bet (ii)	$-q$	$1-q$
net	$1-p-q$	$1-p-q$

Table 2

Coherence also makes c/b ratios satisfy other rules given in chapter 1.VIII, notably

(1.10)   all necessary propositions have probability 1, and
(1.11)   all impossible propositions have probability 0.

For since a necessary proposition A cannot be false, and an impossible proposition B cannot be true, not even hypothetical bets on ¬A and on B could be won, unlike bets on the contingent generalisation

(3.1) $\forall x(Fx \rightarrow Gx)$

considered in section II. That is why coherence requires c/b ratios for bets on any impossible ¬A or B to be zero. And since, as we have just seen, it also requires c/b ratios for bets on any A and ¬A to add up to 1, it also requires c/b ratios to be 1 for bets on any necessary proposition.

Similarly for the other rules given in chapter 1.VIII: coherence can be shown to make c/b ratios satisfy all of them. This is what gives degrees of belief measured by coherent c/b ratios a probability measure, thereby making them what I am calling credences.

Note, however, that Dutch Book arguments do not show that your c/b ratios *will* be coherent and will therefore be probabilities: merely that, if they are not, you have missed the point of betting. For this reason coherence is usually taken to constrain not our *actual* c/b ratios, and hence our actual degrees of belief, but the degrees of belief we *should* have if we are rational, on the grounds that it is irrational to accept bets we are certain to lose whatever happens.

This view of coherence is debatable, since it need not be irrational to accept c/b ratios that are not probabilities. For example, it is not irrational for book-makers to offer – and for their clients to accept – ratios for bets on horses winning a race that add up to more than 1; since bookmakers make their living partly from the profits this incoherence gives them. More to the point, it would not be irrational for a charitable bookmaker to give away money by making deserving clients accept ratios that add up to *less* than 1. In short, and in general, there is no obvious rational objection to my offering or accepting bets which I know will certainly result in my losing money to a good cause.

I think the real objection to incoherent c/b ratios is not that they are irrational, but that their incoherence stops them being accurate measures of degrees of belief. We saw in section II how factors other than my degree of belief in A can affect the c/b ratios I will accept for bets on A: hence the need to impose conditions on the hypothetical betting situation, to try and stop them doing so. But bookmakers, charitable or not, do not meet these conditions since, as we have noted, the odds they offer for bets are affected by factors other than their degrees of belief that they will win those bets. And similarly in other cases: it is arguable that whenever we knowingly accept an incoherent betting quotient, our decision to accept it is affected by factors other than how strongly we believe that we will win the bet. If this is so, then incoherence in our c/b ratios need not imply incoherence in our degrees of belief.

The claim that our beliefs come by probabilistic degrees may be defended in this way against many apparent counter-examples. Yet this defence must have limits: if the claim is to have any empirical content, it must be capable of empirical refutation. To see how, let us return to the comparison with Newtonian mechanics drawn in chapter 4.IV.

IV

Approximate Credences

Newton's mechanics is an empirical theory that could be – since it has been – shown to be false. In particular, its assumption that the inertial masses of objects remain constant as the objects accelerate is false. For even neglecting relativistic effects, forces applied to objects often knock bits off them, thus reducing their effective inertial mass, while objects that accelerate in air generally drag some air along with them, thus increasing their effective mass. This means that different net forces will make any given object accelerate as if it had slightly different masses, so that the mathematically convenient assumption that the masses of objects have precise values is a theoretical idealisation, an obvious falsehood which no one in practice either believes or needs to use. Yet for most objects at most speeds, the statement in chapter 4.IV of the law linking the acceleration A of a fixed mass M acted on by a net force F,

(5.2) $A = F/M$,

is accurate enough. If it were not, and most objects did not accelerate in a nearly constant proportion to the net forces acting on them, we should have to give up Newton's theory entirely.

But as most objects do accelerate nearly as Newton's theory says, we can still use the theory for most purposes. And whenever we *do* use it, we must take A, F and M to satisfy (5.2), because (5.2) is what tells us *which* acceleration A a force F will cause when applied to a mass M. That is why, in any Newtonian explanation of acceleration, any apparent failure to conform to (5.2) must be attributed to other factors: an unknown force, an unexpected loss or gain of mass – in short, to anything but a failure of the law that gives the explanation its content.

Similarly with the claim that our degrees of belief dispose us to accept only coherent c/b ratios. This too is false, since we often bet incoherently. Yet quite often the claim is, like Newton's theory, a good approximation to the truth, at least of our beliefs in contingent propositions, any one of which can be coherently believed to any degree. It is our degrees of belief in these propositions that are often coherent enough to provide an approximate probability measure of them. And whenever, rightly or wrongly, we use this measure to explain c/b ratios, we must accept the coherence that it assumes; just as users of Newton's theory must accept its measures of force and mass. That is why, in using degrees of belief in contingent propositions to explain betting behaviour, we should ascribe any apparent failure of coherence to other factors: a desire to give money to charity, a reluctance to bet at high c/b ratios or for large stakes, etc., etc. – in short, to anything but a failure of the coherence that gives this kind of explanation of c/b ratios its content.

Another way of resisting apparent counter-examples to coherence is to claim that part of what it *is* to have degrees of belief in contingent propositions is to be disposed to bet coherently at corresponding ratios. This is an application of the thesis that explaining actions in terms of beliefs and desires is *rationalising* them, so that the assumptions these explanations rely on are not just empirical but *constitutive*. Applied to degrees of belief, this thesis turns coherence into a principle which constrains the degrees of belief that we can ascribe to people if we are to make sense of their betting behaviour.

However, not all the consequences of coherence can be defended in this way. Take the consequence noted in section III, that credences satisfy (1.10) and (1.11), i.e. that we all fully believe all necessary propositions and fully disbelieve all impossible ones. This, to put it mildly, is not obviously part of our conception of belief. It does not for example seem irrational or conceptually impossible to doubt or disbelieve a mathematical necessity such as 'There is no greatest prime number' before it has been proved. Nor is it easy to argue that, if this proposition cannot be false, then an English speaker who appears to doubt it must really be doubting a different proposition, namely that the *sentence* S, 'There is no greatest prime number', expresses a necessary truth. For this argument implies that, given what S means, then either it is contingent that the proposition which the sentence S expresses is necessary, or anyone who doubts that S is true must have misunderstood it; and neither view is easy to maintain.

Moreover, even if some such defence of (1.10) works for the necessary truths of logic and mathematics, which are knowable *a priori*, it can hardly work for such allegedly necessary truths as 'Water is H_2O'. For since these are not supposed to be knowable *a priori*, doubt or disbelief in them cannot always be attributed to a failure to grasp them, as Kripke (1972) makes clear in another case:

> We need not ever assume that the biologist's denial that whales are fish shows his 'concept of fishhood' to be different from that of the layman; he simply corrects the layman, discovering that 'whales are mammals, not fish' is a necessary truth. Neither 'whales are mammals' *nor* 'whales are fish' was supposed to be *a priori* or analytic in any case. (p. 330)

If this is right, then laymen who 'incoherently' believe the impossible proposition that whales are fish need be neither irrational nor conceptually confused: they may simply be ill-informed.

While the idea that propositions whose truth cannot be known *a priori* can still be metaphysically necessary may be contentious, it is not so incredible that advocates of credences can afford to rule it out. I conclude therefore that they should not interpret the coherence they need to assume as a requirement of rationality. Rather, they should treat it like Newton's hypothesis that inertial masses are not altered by forces applied to them: that is, as a hypothesis which, although false in general, is close enough to the truth to be useful in many important applications, in this case to our degrees of belief in the contingent propositions on which many of our actions clearly depend.

So understood, much of the predictive inadequacy of both these hypotheses can be accommodated by not ascribing excessively precise values to the quantities they postulate. Thus suppose in Newton's case that applying forces to objects never alters their masses (e.g. by knocking bits off them) by more than, say, 0.1%. Then provided we never credit these objects with masses more precise than that, (5.2)'s correspondingly imprecise predictions of how any net forces will accelerate them can all be true.

Similarly with credences, when coherence does not require them to be 0 or 1. In between, crediting me with a credence of, say, $0.67723\ldots$ in a contingent proposition A may well be absurd; but no more so than crediting me with a mass of $70.523312\ldots$ kilogrammes. And just as I may still have a mass of 70.5 (i.e. of 70.50 ± 0.05) kilogrammes, so I may still have a credence in A of, say, 0.7, i.e. of 0.70 ± 0.05, and hence – in order to satisfy (1.5) precisely – a credence in ¬A of 0.3, i.e. of 0.30 ± 0.05.

This imprecision in the credences, masses and other quantities that things and people have is rarely made explicit. Instead, it is conveniently and conventionally implicit, as I have indicated, in the number of significant figures used to give their values. I emphasise this fact because, if it is overlooked, the literal falsity of seemingly precise ascriptions of credence might well discredit the whole concept. Whereas, once we recognise it, we can see that the imprecision of our credences is no more discreditable than imprecision in the values of instances of any other continuous quantity.

This is not to deny that most of our credences have far less precise values than most masses and temperatures do. An object's mass can often be truly stated to many significant figures, whereas few unconditional credences between 0 and 1 can be stated to more than two. But this matters less than it might, because most of the decisions and actions we use credences to explain are qualitative. This fact is obscured by my taking your credence in a proposition A to be measured by the greatest c/b ratio you would accept for a bet on A in certain conditions, since that is a quantitative question. But that is not the question which faces us in most real betting situations, where the decision we must make is qualitative: for example, whether to accept a c/b ratio of, say, 0.2, offered by a bookmaker for a bet on Pink Gin winning the Derby. We do not need a very precise credence in this proposition to make *that* decision: all we need is a credence whose value is definitely greater or definitely less than 0.2.

V

Decision Theory

If the arguments of section IV do not make the existence of credences undeniable, they do show that the idea of credence is tenable, and it is certainly useful and widely held. And that, as we noted in section I, is good enough for us. Its most important application lies in its role in the so-called *subjective decision theory* mentioned in chapter 1.IV, a theory which, by generalising our betting measure of belief, shows how that measure can be applied more widely and naturally than our discussion of it so far might suggest.

To see how the theory does this, consider Ramsey's (1926) observation that

> all our lives we are in a sense betting. Whenever we go to the station we are betting that a train will really run, and if we had not a sufficient degree of belief in this we should decline the bet and stay at home. (p. 79)

Here the *cost* of the bet is the cost to us in time or money of going to the station, and the *benefit* of winning it is the benefit to us of catching our train.

In this as in many other cases neither the cost of a bet nor the benefit of winning it has to be in cash. It can be in any goods, physical or mental, which we might exchange for a sufficiently enticing prospect of other such goods. For however hard it may be to compare the intrinsic qualities of goods – how does fun or good food compare with art or good company? – we may still measure their value to us by which we prefer when we have to choose between them. This is why what we will pay for things that we *can* buy is often a fair measure of how much we value them, since we will generally pay more for things we prefer.

Still, as the train example shows, the real point of a bet lies in the values to us of its cost and of its benefit, whether or not these values are, or can be, measured in money terms. Decision theory takes these values – our *subjective utilities* – to measure the strength of our *desires*, in this case our desires (a) to catch a train and

(b) not to go to the station if it does not run, just as it takes our credences to measure the strength of our beliefs, such as our belief that the train will run.

Decision theory generalises betting in another way too, which the train case does not illustrate. For there, as in ordinary betting, we cannot get the benefit without paying the cost. That is, we cannot catch the train without going to the station, just as we cannot win bets we have not paid to make. But this is not always so. Suppose you are wondering whether to stop smoking, which you enjoy, to avoid getting cancer, and think of it as a bet: the cost being the value to you of smoking and the benefit being the value to you of not getting cancer. Now this is a benefit that you *might* get without paying the cost, since not all smokers get cancer. Yet since you know that a far higher fraction of smokers than of non-smokers get cancer, your credence in A, that you will avoid cancer, will be greater if you stop smoking (B) than if you carry on (¬B); and this may make you decide to stop, i.e. to make B true. Then decision theory, read descriptively, tells us how your decision will depend on these two possible values of your credence in A, which I shall write '$CR_B(A)$' and '$CR_{\neg B}(A)$' respectively, and the subjective utilities for you of the four possible outcomes B∧A, B∧¬A, ¬B∧A and ¬B∧¬A.

To show what the theory says about all this, I shall make a few simplifying assumptions which, while they are not essential, and often do not hold, may well hold here and will not affect the points I need to make. The first assumption is that the question for you is not whether to smoke less, and if so how much less, but whether to stop completely or to carry on as at present. This makes the decision-making situation a simple choice between two alternatives. My other assumptions, made only to simplify the exposition, are that the cost c to you of stopping smoking will be the same whether or not you get cancer, that the benefit b to you of avoiding cancer will be the same whether you smoke or not, that b and c are both positive, and that b is greater than c.

On these assumptions, your net subjective utilities, relative to what we may call the *default outcome*, ¬B∧¬A, where, by continuing to smoke (¬B) and getting cancer (¬A), you avoid both the cost c and the benefit b, are

$$SU(B \wedge A) = b - c,$$
$$SU(B \wedge \neg A) = -c,$$
$$SU(\neg B \wedge A) = b \text{ and}$$
$$SU(\neg B \wedge \neg A) = 0.$$

These are shown in Table 3 in the more usual form of a *subjective utility matrix*:

The utility for you	if A	if ¬A
of B	$b-c$	$-c$
of ¬B	b	0

Table 3

On their own, however, these utilities will not determine whether you will stop smoking, i.e. will make B true. That will also depend on how likely you think you are to avoid cancer if you do stop and if you do not. That is, it will also depend on your credences $CR_B(A) = p$ and $CR_{\neg B}(A) = p'$, as shown in Table 4.

Your credence	in A	in ¬A
if B	p	$1-p$
if ¬B	p'	$1-p'$

Table 4

Subjective decision theory then uses the data in Tables 3 and 4 to rank B and ¬B by their *expected* utilities, defined as follows. B's expected subjective utility for you, $ESU(B)$, is the average of $SU(B \wedge A)$ and $SU(B \wedge \neg A)$, B's actual subjective utilities for you if A is true and if ¬A is, weighted respectively by the credences $CR_B(A)$ and $CR_B(\neg A)$ that you will have in A if you believe B is true, so that

(5.3) $\quad ESU(B) = [CR_B(A) \times SU(B \wedge A)] + [CR_B(\neg A) \times SU(B \wedge \neg A)]$
$\qquad\qquad = p(b-c) + (1-p)(-c)$
$\qquad\qquad = pb - c.$

Similarly the expected subjective utility of ¬B is

(5.4) $\quad ESU(\neg B) = [CR_{\neg B}(A) \times SU(\neg B \wedge A)] + [CR_{\neg B}(\neg A) \times SU(\neg B \wedge \neg A)]$
$\qquad\qquad = p'b.$

Then the theory's *principle of maximising expected subjective utility* (PMESU), read descriptively, says that you will stop smoking, i.e. make B true, if

$\qquad ESU(B) > ESU(\neg B)$, i.e. if
$\qquad (pb - c) > p'b$, i.e. if
$\qquad p - p' > c/b.$

In words: the theory says that you *will* make B true if (you think) your credence in A if you do make B true will exceed your credence in A if you make ¬B true by more than your c/b ratio, i.e. by more than the ratio of the cost to you of making B true to the benefit to you if A is true.

Similarly, the theory says that you will carry on smoking, i.e. make ¬B true, if

$\qquad ESU(B) < ESU(\neg B)$, i.e. if
$\qquad p - p' < c/b,$

while if

$\qquad ESU(B) = ESU(\neg B)$, i.e. if
$\qquad p - p' = c/b,$

the theory says nothing either way.

Note that in the special case of ordinary bets, where, if A is 'you win' and B is 'you bet', $p' = 0$ – because you know you cannot win unless you bet – the theory says that you will not bet unless

$\qquad p \geq c/b,$

i.e. unless your credence in A if you bet is at least equal to your c/b ratio for the bet. In other words, the greatest c/b ratio or betting quotient you will accept for a bet is, as we noted in section II, equal to your degree of belief if you bet, that you will win.

The above is the merest sketch of subjective decision theory, to which there is much more than I have indicated. Here however I need to make just two more points about it. First, I have stated the theory as if it inferred decisions from utilities, when in fact the inference usually goes the other way. The theory is generally used to infer utilities from decisions, just as in section II we inferred credences from greatest acceptable c/b ratios. The inference here is more complicated, since it has to disentangle, in ways that we need not go into, the contributions made to our decisions by our utilities on the one hand and by our credences on the other. But the basic idea is the same: our decisions measure our utilities, just as our greatest acceptable c/b ratios measure our credences.

Here again, however, we must distinguish inference from explanation, as we did in noting in section II how temperatures are inferred from the thermometer readings they explain. Inference and explanation there go in opposite directions, as they do in quantitative measurement generally, including that of credences by c/b ratios. We postulate credences to explain why people accept some c/b ratios and not others, while inferring those credences from the very ratios they explain. Similarly in subjective decision theory's simultaneous postulation of credences and utilities to explain the decisions we use to measure them. There is no more mystery or circularity in this than in the measurement of any other physical or psychological quantity.

The second point I need to make about subjective decision theory is this. I have stated its key principle, PMESU, of maximising subjective expected utility, as a *descriptive* thesis, about how people do act under uncertainty. Most decision theorists, however, take PMESU to be not descriptive but *normative*. That is, they take PMESU to say not how we *do* act but how it is *rational* for us to act on our utilities and credences. They do this for the reason, criticised in section III, that coherence is taken to be a criterion of rationality, namely that, as a descriptive claim, it faces too many counter-examples: we too often accept incoherent c/b ratios. Similarly, too many people acting under uncertainty seem not to maximise their subjective expected utility, thus falsifying PMESU as a descriptive thesis.

I said in section III why I prefer to read coherence as a false but often predictively useful descriptive thesis than as a requirement of rationality. Since PMESU entails coherence, I take the same view of it: as a descriptive theory of how we actually act under uncertainty which, while often false, is also often close enough to the truth to be a useful approximation to it.

This in particular lets me draw a simple distinction between the credence we *actually* have in any contingent proposition A and the credence we *should* have in A given our evidence about A. For even if rationality sets no limits to the former, it may well set limits to the latter. Those who take credences to measure rational rather than actual degrees of belief must draw this distinction differently. For them the distinction is between the principles of rationality that are needed for coherence, and therefore for the ascription of credences, and further, epistemic, principles that limit the credences which evidence about a proposition A makes it rational for someone with that evidence to have in A.

This question, about how and why our credences in contingent propositions should be constrained by evidence, is the key question of our next chapter, on epistemic probability. In discussing that question I shall, for simplicity, write as if ascriptions of actual credences are purely descriptive, as indeed I think they are. Those who think otherwise will have to read my question, of whether evidence imposes *any* rational constraints on credences, as the question of whether it imposes any *additional* constraints, over and above those needed to make degrees of belief credences in the first place. However, since it will make no odds to the ensuing discussion which way the question is put, I shall feel free in what follows to take my way of putting it, and hence the purely factual existence of actual credences, for granted.

Further Reading

Ramsey (1926) is the classic source for the subjective interpretation of probability, and of the Dutch Book argument for a probability measure of degrees of belief. It is reprinted in Kyburg (1964), which also contains much other useful material, notably Venn's (1888) attack on subjectivism and de Finetti's seminal (1937). For more arguments against crediting people with precise credences, see Levi (1980), chapters 4 and 9.

For the view that there are necessary truths which cannot be known *a priori*, see Kripke (1980). For the thesis that our actions are explained by our beliefs and desires, and that this fact is constitutive of our concepts of belief, desire and action, see Davidson (1970).

For more detailed accounts of the so-called 'non-causal' kind of decision theory outlined above, see Jeffrey (1983), and Eells (1982). Besides the non-causal theories of Ramsey, Savage and Jeffrey, the latter also discusses the causal decision theories of Gibbard and Harper, Skyrms, and Lewis. For a good collection of articles on decision theory, game theory and rational action in general, see Moser (1990).

6
Confirmation

I

Measuring Evidential Support

Having examined chance and credence at some length, we now turn to the third, *epistemic*, kind of probability introduced in chapter 1. This is the kind that is meant to measure 'how far evidence supports or counts against various hypotheses about the world, for example that our world had a beginning or that the butler did it'.

Quantitative theories of evidential support are commonly called *confirmation theories*. Although these are not all *probabilistic* (i.e. use a probability measure), I shall only discuss those that are. This is partly on the grounds, given in chapter 1.IX, that philosophical issues about evidence show up equally well in probabilistic and non-probabilistic theories. But there is also a positive reason for using a probability measure of evidential support, or confirmation.

Suppose we can discover, never mind how, whether and roughly to what extent some evidence B confirms a contingent proposition A. Now consider what I shall call the *evidence-to-credence principle* (EC), that

(EC) the more B confirms A, the greater the degree of belief in A which B justifies.

This allows us – although it does not force us – to equate *degrees of confirmation of A* with *justified degrees of belief in A*. By so doing, it lets us use the degree of belief in A which B justifies to measure how far B confirms A. And then, since we already know from chapter 5 that degrees of belief have a probability measure, this gives us a probability measure of confirmation.

Why should we accept (EC)? One reason is that it gives confirmation a pragmatic point which it would otherwise lack. For what after all does knowing how much B confirms A tell us? We know that, if B confirms A strongly enough, it tells us that we may infer A from B. But what if B confirms A too weakly to justify inferring A and too strongly to justify inferring ¬A? What are we to do with such inconclusive evidence? To that question the merely qualitative concepts of full belief in A, or in ¬A, and of inferring one of these from B, offer no answer. But the quantitative concept of degrees of belief does, via the subjective decision theory outlined in chapter 5.V.

This decision theory says how our actions either are or should be affected not only by what we believe but by how strongly we believe it, i.e. by our credences. The theory may, as we have noted, be read either descriptively or normatively. That is, it may be taken to say how, given our subjective utilities, our credences *do* make us act, or how they *would* make us act if we were rational. On the descriptive reading, rationality is an extra constraint, which tells us what to do by telling us what credences we should have given our evidence. But even on the normative reading, rationality may still provide extra constraints over and above those that justify the theory itself. That is, even if it is always rational to act as the theory says on our *actual* credences, our actions will be better still if the credences we act on are justified by our evidence. This is the pragmatic content which our decision theory enables (EC) to give to evidential support: in justifying a certain credence, our evidence thereby justifies the actions which that credence would or should combine with (justified) subjective utilities to cause.

This is the positive argument for letting the $CR(A)$ which evidence B justifies provide a probability measure of how far B confirms A, by identifying that $CR(A)$ with the epistemic probability $EP(A \mid B)$. The argument is not uncontentious; but for present purposes it does not need to be. For the most important question about a supposed quantitative relation of confirmation is not whether we should use probability to measure it, but whether any such relation exists. That is the question we must now consider, and it will not be begged by our taking a probability measure of it for granted.

II

Epistemic and Other Probabilities

Epistemic probabilities, if there are any, differ in two main ways from credences and chances. First, they express *relations* between two propositions, one being a hypothesis, the other being, if true, evidence for or against that hypothesis (or evidentially neutral). In the terminology of chapter 1.VII, these probabilities are essentially *conditional*, which credences and chances need not be. Hence the different symbolism: '$CR(A)$' for a credence in A, '$CH(A)$' for a chance of A, and '$EP(A \mid B)$' for A's epistemic probability given evidence B.

The essentially relational nature of epistemic probabilities gives the question of 'how far evidence confirms or disconfirms' a proposition A an ambiguity that needs to be resolved. We may want to know whether and how much A is, on balance, confirmed by all the evidence we have; or we may want to know whether and how much a given piece of evidence confirms A. Each reading of the question raises two issues which we must now settle before we proceed.

Starting with the first reading, suppose in our horse-racing example that proposition A says that Pink Gin will win the Derby, B says that he is the favourite and C says that he has been lame. This gives A three possible epistemic probabilities: $\text{EP}(A\,|\,B)$, $\text{EP}(A\,|\,C)$ and $\text{EP}(A\,|\,B\wedge C)$, which may well have different values. Which of them, if any, measures the strength of our evidence for or against A?

The standard answer is given by the so-called *total evidence principle*: measure A's confirmation by its epistemic probability conditional on *all* the evidence about it that we have or can get. In our case, this rules out $\text{EP}(A\,|\,B)$ and $\text{EP}(A\,|\,C)$. But it does not rule $\text{EP}(A\,|\,B\wedge C)$ *in*, since even $B\wedge C$ is not *all* our evidence about A. We have a mass of other background evidence, ranging from facts about horses in general and Pink Gin in particular, through facts about the state of the course, to facts about sunlight, turf and gravity, all of which are part of our evidence about A. So if we call all this background evidence K, what really measures A's overall confirmation is $\text{EP}(A\,|\,K\wedge B\wedge C)$ or, in general, $\text{EP}(A\,|\,E_T)$, where E_T is the conjunction of all the evidence about A that is available to us.

This reference to evidence 'that is available to us' is admittedly vague, but not so vague as to make the total evidence principle useless. For first, since all our empirical evidence comes ultimately from perception, and no one can perceive today what will happen tomorrow, E_T is always apt to change, and so therefore is A's overall evidential support. The other reason E_T's vagueness matters less than it might is that the value of $\text{EP}(A\,|\,E_T)$, which is what does matter, may not vary much with changes in E_T produced by changes in the evidence available to us: in particular, it may not vary enough to affect whether E_T supports A.

This brings us to the other issue here, namely *how* the value of $\text{EP}(A\,|\,E_T)$ determines whether or not E_T confirms A. Assuming that evidence disconfirms A just in case it confirms its negation, $\neg A$, we may take it that E_T confirms A if and only if $\text{EP}(A\,|\,E_T)$ is greater than $\text{EP}(\neg A\,|\,E_T)$, and hence that

E_T confirms A if $\text{EP}(A\,|\,E_T) > 1/2 > \text{EP}(\neg A\,|\,E_T)$,
E_T confirms $\neg A$ if $\text{EP}(A\,|\,E_T) < 1/2 < \text{EP}(\neg A\,|\,E_T)$, and
E_T confirms neither A nor $\neg A$ if $\text{EP}(A\,|\,E_T) = \text{EP}(\neg A\,|\,E_T) = 1/2$.

This shows how much new evidence may need to change $\text{EP}(A\,|\,E_T)$ to make E_T cease to confirm A (or $\neg A$), or even to make it confirm A or $\neg A$ weakly rather than strongly, which is often all we want to know. This is why E_T's vagueness is often immaterial, and also why we rarely want to know how *much* E_T confirms A, something that could in principle be measured by (e.g.) the difference

$$\text{EP}(A\,|\,E_T) - \text{EP}(\neg A\,|\,E_T).$$

On the other reading of our question – whether a specific piece of evidence B confirms a proposition A – its answer depends on a quite different comparison, noted at the end of chapter 1.VII. The question now is not whether an E_T which includes B makes $\text{EP}(A\,|\,E_T)$ greater than $\text{EP}(\neg A\,|\,E_T)$ but whether including B in E_T *raises* $\text{EP}(A\,|\,E_T)$: i.e., if K is our background evidence, whether $\text{EP}(A\,|\,K\wedge B)$ is greater than $\text{EP}(A\,|\,K)$. If it is, then B confirms A, even if $\text{EP}(A\,|\,K\wedge B)$ is less than $1/2$, as the example of smoking and cancer shows. For if A is someone's getting cancer and B is their smoking, we take B to confirm A because, since cancer is more common in smokers than in the population at large, we take $\text{EP}(A\,|\,K\wedge B)$ to be greater than $\text{EP}(A \mid K)$. And we do so even though, because most smokers die of something else before they get cancer, $\text{EP}(A \mid K \wedge B)$ is less than $\text{EP}(\neg A \mid K \wedge B)$ and therefore less than $1/2$.

In general, then, since B will raise A's epistemic probability if and only if it lowers $\neg$A's, we may assume that

> B confirms A if $\text{EP}(A \mid K \wedge B) > \text{EP}(A \mid K)$,
> B disconfirms A if $\text{EP}(A \mid K \wedge B) < \text{EP}(A \mid K)$, and
> B is evidentially irrelevant to A if $\text{EP}(A \mid K \wedge B) = \text{EP}(A \mid K)$.

III

Inductive Logic

The fact that epistemic probabilities are relative to evidence is not the only way in which they differ from credences and chances. From credences they also differ in not being *subjective*. By 'subjective' I mean that there is no contradiction in two people, or one person at two times, having quite different credences in any given proposition A. But two people who, for any given A and B, credit $\text{EP}(A \mid B)$ with incompatible values do contradict each other, just as they do if they credit a given chance $\text{CH}(A)$ with incompatible values: in each case one of them at least must be wrong.

If the objectivity of epistemic probabilities makes them resemble chances in one way, they differ from chances in another way by not being empirical. To see why not, suppose proposition A says that a coin toss's chance $\text{CH}(H)$ of landing heads is less than 0.5, B says that 15 out of 100 similar tosses landed heads, and $\text{EP}(A \mid K \wedge B)$ has the value 0.9, where K is our background evidence. Then while the proposition A, that $\text{CH}(H) < 0.5$, may well have an epistemic probability given $K \wedge B$, the proposition '$\text{EP}(A \mid K \wedge B) = 0.9$', which says what this epistemic probability is, has no epistemic probabilities at all – or at least none that can differ relative to different propositions. The reason is that, as $\text{EP}(A \mid K \wedge B)$, if it exists, will be a *relation* between A and $K \wedge B$, additional evidence C will not be evidence for or against '$\text{EP}(A \mid K \wedge B) = 0.9$': it will simply define a quite different epistemic probability, $\text{EP}(A \mid K \wedge B \wedge C)$, relating A to the conjunction $K \wedge B \wedge C$. This is the sense in which epistemic probabilities, unlike chances, are not empirical. For if they themselves have no – or no usefully variable – epistemic probabilities, empirical data cannot provide evidence for or against them by making hypotheses about their values more or less probable.

Yet how, if not by being empirical, can epistemic probabilities be objective? The usual answer is: by being *logical*. Compare the logical relation of *entailment*, like the entailment that links B to its deductive consequences, such as the disjunction $B \vee A$. This is a very paradigm of an objective but non-empirical relation between propositions. It is also evidential, since it makes B conclusive evidence for any contingent proposition it entails. Hence the view that epistemic probabilities are logical relations and that a confirmation theory simply extends the deductive logic of *conclusive* evidence to a logic of *inconclusive* evidence.

The basic idea is this. A system of deductive logic is one for which it can be shown that inferences of the forms it endorses are deductively valid: that is, it is not possible for all their premises to be true and their conclusions false. Thus in a deductive system which endorses Modus Ponens (MP),

B	premise
$\underline{B \to A}$	premise
A	conclusion,

where '_ →...' means 'if _ then ...', (MP) is deductively valid. This is why if all the premises of such an inference are known to be true, they are conclusive evidence for its conclusion.

As a theory of evidence, however, deductive logic is seriously incomplete, because our evidence for contingent propositions rarely if ever entails them. A complete theory of evidence must therefore also tell us what makes inferences reasonable when their premises do *not* entail their conclusions. Hence the idea of *inductive* logic, so-called because the philosophical problem of induction is to say what makes some such inferences reasonable, like that from 'the sun has risen every day so far' to 'the sun will rise tomorrow' or, more ambitiously, to 'the sun will always rise every day'. This is another reason for calling confirmation theories logics: like deductive logics, they are theories of *inference*.

But not *only* of inference, as we noted in section I. For while any proposition A which B entails can safely be inferred from B, that does not follow when evidence B does *not* entail A. This is most obvious when B supports A and ¬A equally, as when A says that a coin toss will land heads and B says that the toss is unbiased, which entitles us to infer neither A nor ¬A. And even if B confirms A slightly, by saying that the toss is biased towards heads, but not much, it will still not entitle us to *infer* A, i.e. to conclude that the coin toss certainly *will* land heads: it will simply justify a somewhat greater credence in A than in ¬A. So confirmation theories, unlike deductive logics, need to cover more than inference if they are to be complete theories of evidential support.

This difference between confirmation theories and deductive logics does not, however, show that the former are not *logics*. What may seem to show this is the difference that generates the problem of induction, namely that inconclusive support is *defeasible* in a way that entailment is not. In denying that entailment is defeasible I mean that evidence B which entails A cannot be outweighed by any further evidence C: for if B entails A, so – via B – will the conjunction B∧C. Evidence for a contingent A which does not entail A, on the other hand, can *always* be outweighed by new evidence. Thus in the sunrise case, however strongly B ('the sun has risen every day so far') confirms A ('the sun will always rise every day'), A can still be falsified by new evidence C ('the sun fails to rise tomorrow'). Hence the problem of induction.

The defeasibility of non-deductive support may seem to threaten its logical status by showing that it, and hence the epistemic probabilities which measure it, are contingent after all. Take the horse-racing case of section II where, besides the background evidence K, two pieces of evidence are relevant to the proposition A that Pink Gin will win the Derby: B, that he is the favourite, which confirms A; and C, that he has been lame, which disconfirms A. This appears to make $EP(A \mid K \wedge B)$ contingent on C's truth, by making its value less if C is true than if C is false. This suggests that, in general, $EP(A \mid K \wedge B)$ is contingent on C just in case

(i) $EP(A \mid K \wedge B) = EP(A \mid K \wedge B \wedge C)$ if C,
(ii) $EP(A \mid K \wedge B) = EP(A \mid K \wedge B \wedge \neg C)$ if $\neg C$, and
(iii) $EP(A \mid K \wedge B \wedge C) \neq EP(A \mid K \wedge B \wedge \neg C)$.

This is certainly the sense in which entailment is never contingent on any C: for, as we have noted, if B entails A, so will any conjunction that contains B, as both $K \wedge B \wedge C$ and $K \wedge B \wedge \neg C$ do.

It is therefore as well for the idea of inductive logic that, appearances to the contrary, epistemic probabilities are *not* contingent in this sense. This is because, as we noted in section II, evidence C does not *alter* $EP(A \mid K \wedge B)$: that epistemic probability will be the same whether C is true or false. All C does is give A the distinct epistemic probability $EP(A \mid K \wedge B \wedge C)$. So if clause (iii) in our definition of contingency is true, then at least one and usually both of the clauses (i) and (ii) will be false: since if $EP(A \mid K \wedge B \wedge C) \neq EP(A \mid K \wedge B \wedge \neg C)$, $EP(A \mid K \wedge B)$ usually lies between them. Thus in our horse-racing example, where B confirms A, and C disconfirms it, the relevant epistemic probabilities, if they exist, might be

$$EP(A \mid K \wedge B \wedge C) = 0.5,$$
$$EP(A \mid K \wedge B \wedge \neg C) = 0.7 \text{ and}$$
$$EP(A \mid K \wedge B) = 0.6,$$

regardless of whether A, B, C or any other empirical proposition is true; and likewise in other cases. For no A and B will $EP(A \mid K \wedge B)$, if it exists, be any more contingent on any other empirical fact than entailment is.

IV

Chances as Evidence

Despite the arguments of section III, the logical status of epistemic probabilities may still be denied on the grounds that, unlike the truths of a deductive logic, we cannot know them *a priori*. However, while that may be true, what matters here is not whether we should call epistemic probabilities 'logical', but by what means, *a priori* or otherwise, we can discover their values. For we can only know how probable our total evidence E_T makes A if we know $EP(A \mid E_T)$'s value; just as, with given background evidence K, we can only know whether new evidence B confirms A if we know whether $EP(A \mid K \wedge B)$ is greater than $EP(A \mid K)$.

How then can we discover the values of epistemic probabilities? We need not assume that they relate all propositions A and B: what, for example, is the probability of rain tonight given only that the earth is round? Yet if there are any epistemic probabilities, then if A says that it will rain tonight, $\text{EP}(A|B)$ must surely exist for some meteorological propositions B which entail neither A nor ¬A. But how, if they do, can we learn their values?

We saw in chapter 2.VI that the *a priori* principle of indifference will not help us here: the mere fact that we have no reason either to expect rain or to not expect it does not give rain an epistemic probability $1/2$. Similarly for all other mutually exclusive outcomes, simple or complex, in any sample space: they are not given equal epistemic probabilities by the mere fact that our background evidence K tells us nothing about how probable they are.

Perhaps the least contentious source of epistemic probabilities is what we may call the *chances-as-evidence* principle (C-E), which says that for all A and p,

(C-E) $\text{EP}(A\,|\,\text{CH}(A)=p) = p.$

In words: A's epistemic probability, given only that A has a chance p of being true, is also p. So, for example, the epistemic probability that a coin toss will land heads, given only that its chance of doing so is 0.5, must also be 0.5.

While (C-E) is hard to deny, on any view of chance or epistemic probability, it is not very useful, since rarely if ever is the fact that $\text{CH}(A) = p$ *all* our evidence about A. And when it is not, our other evidence may trump it, most obviously when that evidence includes A itself. For then, because $A \wedge B$ entails A,

$\text{EP}(A\,|\,A\wedge B) = 1$ and $\text{EP}(A\,|\,\neg A\wedge B) = 0$

for all B consistent with A and with ¬A. So in particular, for all p less than 1 and greater than 0,

$\text{EP}(A\,|\,A\wedge\text{CH}(A)=p) = 1$ and $\text{EP}(A\,|\,\neg A\wedge\text{CH}(A)=p) = 0.$

Thus, for example, if A says that a tossed coin lands heads, and I know whether A or ¬A is true because I see how the coin lands, my credence in A must be 1 or 0 even if I also know that $\text{CH}(A) = 0.5$.

Fortunately, this limitation on the use of (C-E) is less severe than it may seem, since we often know $\text{CH}(A)$ before we know whether A is true. This is basically because, as we noted in section II, we cannot see what has not yet happened: we cannot for example see how a tossed coin lands before it does so. So if I know in advance that its chance $\text{CH}(A)$ of landing heads $= p$, this evidence cannot be trumped by the evidence that A is true, or that ¬A is, since that evidence is not then available. Nor, if we assume that effects never precede their causes, can the evidence that $\text{CH}(A)=p$ be trumped by the evidence of any *effects* of A's or of ¬A's being true, since that evidence too will not be available in advance.

It is however not enough to exclude A or ¬A, and their effects, from our evidence when equating A's epistemic probability with its known chance of being true. For while we cannot see in advance either how a coin toss will land or what effects its landing as it does will have, we might see or have other evidence for a 'hidden variable', i.e. some fact about the toss which, with a deterministic law, entails how it will land or even, with a further *in*deterministic law, gives the coin a different chance of landing heads.

Any evidence D for such a conjunction of fact and law must therefore also be excluded from our evidence before we can infer A's epistemic probability from CH(A). But this is not a serious restriction: for even if some such evidence D exists, we rarely know it; and if we did, we would not be inferring A's epistemic probability from CH(A) anyway. This being so, we might perhaps take D's exclusion for granted, as we might that of A, ¬A and their effects. And where these are the only sources of evidence about A, available in advance, that might trump our knowledge of its chance, we may replace (C-E) above with the rather more useful 'chances-as-evidence' principle (CE) that

(CE) $EP(A \mid K \wedge CH(A)=p) = p$,

where our background evidence K – available before either A or ¬A is – includes no evidence for a value of CH(A) other than p.

However, even if (CE) faces no other objections, its utility will still be limited by the difficulty of telling whether a largely unarticulated K contains evidence for another value of CH(A). The most that can be said for (CE) is that, for any given value of p, it will remain true for a much wider range of propositions K than will any

$EP(A \mid K \wedge B) = p$

where B does *not* credit A with a chance p of being true.

Moreover, even where (CE) applies, it can only fix A's epistemic probability if CH(A) is fixed by something else, e.g. by a statistical law. Take the law of radio-activity discussed in chapters 3.III and 4.IV. This says that the chance p_t of radium atoms decaying within any period of t years is $1-e^{-\lambda t}$, where λ is a constant. This, plus (CE), entails that the epistemic probability that any atom a will decay within t years, given this law and the fact that a is a radium atom, is $1-e^{-\lambda t}$. Similarly in other cases. For any F and G, if a law, stated by a proposition L, gives F-things a chance p of being G, (CE) tells us that the epistemic probability of any object a being G, given L and the fact that a is F, is also p:

(6.1) $EP(Ga \mid L \wedge Fa) = p$.

The epistemic probability in (6.1) is however still conditional on the chance p that an F-thing is G, since it is conditional on the proposition L which says what that chance is. But now suppose we make the – controversial – assumption that L is a necessary truth, i.e. that the law which L states holds in all possible worlds. If it does, L will imply nothing about which possible world is actual, nor therefore about which contingent propositions are actually true. In short, like all other necessary – e.g. logical or mathematical – truths, L will be evidentially vacuous: adding or subtracting it from the evidence about any contingent proposition will not alter that proposition's epistemic probability. So if L *is* necessary, (6.1) will entail

(6.2) $EP(Ga \mid Fa) = p$,

an equation which does not refer to chances at all.

Equation (6.2) in effect reinterprets the chance p as an epistemic probability, an interpretation which, philosophers may note, offers a natural extension of Hume's view that causation is the sole basis of our non-deductive inferences. To see why it does this, recall from chapter 3.III that, on a Humean (i.e. frequency) reading of chances, the real form of the law L is

$$f(Gx/Fx) = p,$$

where $f(Gx/Fx)$ is the relative frequency among F-things of those that are G. This offers a natural weakening of Hume's requirement that causes be 'constantly conjoined' with their effects, meaning that being F causes F-things to be G only if *all* F's are G, i.e. only if the relative frequency $f(Gx/Fx) = 1$. Similarly, on the rival propensity view of chance discussed in chapter 4.IV, statistical laws of the form

$$\forall x(Fx \rightarrow \text{CH}(Gx)=p)$$

offer a natural weakening of deterministic laws of the form $\forall x(Fx \rightarrow \text{CH}(Gx)=1)$.

Thus on both these views of chance, a statistical weakening of the claim that causes determine their effects lets the idea that something like (CE) is our sole source of epistemic probabilities express Hume's thesis that 'all our reasonings concerning matters of fact ... are founded on the relation of cause and effect' (Hume 1748, sect. IV, §28). This thesis is also consistent with the assumption, needed to derive (6.2) from (6.1), that L is a necessary truth. We noted in chapter 5.IV the claim of Kripke and others that a law of nature, e.g. that water is H_2O, may be necessary without being knowable *a priori*. If that is so, then L need not be contingent in order for Hume's claim that 'causes and effects are discoverable, not by reason but by experience' (§24) to be as true of indeterministic as of deterministic causation.

V

Confirmation Relations

Unfortunately, using (6.2) to extract epistemic probabilities from statistical laws does not answer the crucial question, posed at the start of section IV, of how to discover their values, since no one thinks that laws of nature can be known *a priori*, even if they hold in all possible worlds. So in order to learn the value p of the epistemic probability in (6.2), we must first discover – 'not by reason but by experience' – the value p of the chance which F-things have of being G. But in that case why postulate epistemic probabilities at all; why not just use the chance p as stated in L to measure directly how strongly the evidence that something is F supports the hypothesis that it is G? The epistemic probability in (6.2) looks more like a gratuitous way of restating this support than a real relation between Fa and Ga, distinct from Ga's chance, on whose existence the support depends.

This is not the only objection to the idea that epistemic probabilities measure a special confirmation relation. Another is that we cannot use epistemic probabilities derived from chances unless those chances can be evidence, i.e. unless we can know what their values are. But how can we know this, given that, as we noted in chapter 1.III, chances are not directly observable? We can observe rain, coin tosses landing heads, radium atoms decaying, people getting cancer, etc., but not the chances, if any, of these happenings. We can only learn the value of a CH(A) by observing some *non*-chance evidence B for it, usually frequency evidence of how often it rains, coin tosses land heads, and so on. But then, before anything like (CE) can tell us A's epistemic probability given that CH(A) = p, we need B to tell us what p is. And for B to tell us that we must know the epistemic probabilities, given B, of various hypotheses about p: probabilities which cannot therefore be instances of (CE). But if we need non-chance evidence about chances, chances cannot provide all the epistemic probabilities whose values we may need to know.

There are also many non-chance propositions for which our evidence need not include chances. Take our initial examples of epistemic probabilities, repeated at the start of this chapter: that the world had a beginning, and that the butler committed the crime. Our evidence about these hypotheses need not give them any chances, i.e. physical probabilities, to which their epistemic probabilities can be equated. For in the first case there may well be no such thing as the *physical* probability of the universe having a beginning; and in the second, as we also noted in 1.III, any chance that the butler *would* do the crime may well differ from the epistemic probability that he *did* do it. Neither in these nor in many other cases is the existence of epistemic probabilities either obvious or inferable from anything else. Only in the special cases discussed in section IV do we have anything like a clear way of discovering epistemic probabilities, and that way makes them redundant, since in those cases chances can do their job for them.

It is for this reason that many philosophers now deny that epistemic probabilities measure a confirmation relation, logical or otherwise, between hypotheses and evidence. This is not to deny that evidence can confirm hypotheses, nor that we can use numerical probabilities to measure that confirmation, and may therefore call those probabilities epistemic. It is only to deny that postulating a special relation helps to explain our use of probability to measure confirmation in the way that, as we saw in sections I and IV, postulating credences and chances may help to explain it, via the principles (EC) and (CE).

Yet how are the undeniable facts of confirmation to be explained, if not by a confirmation relation? One answer lies in the evidence-to-credence principle (EC), i.e. in equating degrees of support for any contingent proposition A with justified degrees of belief in A. This reduces the question of confirmation to the question of how evidence B should constrain our credence in a proposition A: a question which, as we shall see in chapter 7, may be answered without postulating any special evidential relation between A and B.

Further Reading

A classic statement of the logical interpretation of probability is given in chapter 1 of Keynes (1921). For confirmation theory in general, see Kuipers (1998), the papers in Carnap and Jeffrey (1971), and especially Carnap (1971). For a discussion of Carnap's views on logical probability, with plenty of further references, see Hájek (2001).

The principle (C-E) is similar to what Lewis (1980a) calls the *principal principle*. Skyrms (1980) takes what he calls the *resilience* of credences derived from chances that underlies (CE) to provide a subjectivist reduction of chances to resilient credences. (For a discussion of subjective surrogates for chance, see chapter 10 below.)

For the confirmation of scientific theories, see Howson and Urbach (1993), which advocates the Bayesian approach outlined in chapter 7, and Glymour (1980), chapter 3, and Earman (1992), chapters 2–5, which criticise it. See also Salmon (1990), which uses the frequency with which certain hypotheses have been successful to provide an objective basis for judging the plausibility of theories.

7

Conditionalisation

I

Conditional Probability

In this chapter I shall develop a widely-accepted account of how evidence about contingent propositions should affect our credences in them, an account which does not postulate any confirmation relations. It assumes instead that, for all propositions A and B, the conditional probability $P(A \mid B)$ will, on any reading of it, satisfy the equation,

$$(1.2) \quad P(A \mid B) = \frac{P(A \wedge B)}{P(B)},$$

which gives $P(A \mid B)$ a value fixed by the values of the unconditional probabilities $P(A \wedge B)$ and $P(B)$, provided only that $P(B)$ is greater than 0.

It is now time to ask why we should accept (1.2). The usual answer to this question is that it is true by definition, because it defines $P(A \mid B)$. However, this reading of (1.2) does not explain why $P(A \mid B)$ has the implications it was credited with when the concept of conditional probability was introduced in chapter 1.VII. It cannot for example follow just from (1.2) that, as stated in 1.VII, A will be *independent* of B, 'meaning that B tells us nothing about A's prospects of being true,' if and only if $P(A \wedge B)/P(B)$ is equal to A's *un*conditional probability $P(A)$.

More generally and importantly, (1.2) does not entail that, read epistemically, $P(A \mid B)$ measures the credence in A that is justified by learning that B is true. This poses a dilemma. On the one hand, imposing that epistemic entailment makes (1.2) a substantive thesis about conditional probabilities so understood: it can no longer be made true merely by definition. On the other hand, if we use (1.2) to define $P(A \mid B)$, we cannot take its epistemic application for granted, as we have so far done. It may not matter which we do, but we cannot have it both ways. We cannot assume that an epistemic $EP(A \mid B)$ will, by mere definition, both satisfy (1.2) and measure the credence in A which evidence B justifies. We can make $EP(A \mid B)$ do one or the other by definition, but not both: so whichever is not done by definition will have to be argued for.

In this book I shall follow the usual practice of taking equation (1.2), however interpreted, to be true by definition. This makes (1.2) trivially true, while leaving its applications open to question, including its most important and contentious application, the epistemic one. How then are we to justify that application: why should an $EP(A \mid B)$ defined by (1.2) fix the credence we should have in A given evidence B?

II

The Pro Rata Rule

Consider a variant of the die-throwing example used in chapter 2.IV to introduce the terminology of sample spaces. Suppose our background evidence K tells us that a throw of a die will land 1, 2, 3, 4, 5 or 6, and that these six results have the following probabilities (however interpreted):

(7.1) $P[1] = 0.3; P[2] = 0.2; P[3] = 0.1; P[4] = 0.2; P[5] = 0.1; P[6] = 0.1;$

so that, as the rules of numerical probability require,

$$P[1] + P[2] + P[3] + P[4] + P[5] + P[6] = 1.$$

We can take these results to be the sample points of a sample space $\{1,2,3,4,5,6\}$, which in 2.IV I called Ω but will now call the *outcome* and write $\underline{K}$, corresponding to the *proposition* K, the background evidence which tells us (among other things) that the throw of the die will have one and only one of these six results.

Next, let the proposition B say that the result of the throw is an odd number, i.e. is in the set $\{1,3,5\}$ that is the corresponding outcome $\underline{B}$, whose probability in $\underline{K}$ is therefore

(7.2) $P(B) = P\{1,3,5\} = P[1] + P[3] + P[5] = 0.3 + 0.1 + 0.1 = 0.5.$

The information that B is true, and hence that the result of throwing the die is either 1, 3 or 5, turns $\underline{B}$ into a *new* sample space $\{1,3,5\}$ in which 1, 3 and 5 have so-called *posterior* probabilities (so-called because they are posterior to this information), which, using the notation of chapter 5.V, I shall write '$P_B[1]$', '$P_B[3]$' and '$P_B[5]$'. How are these probabilities related to the *prior* probabilities (or *priors*) in $\underline{K}$? They cannot all equal the corresponding priors $P[1]$, $P[3]$ and $P[5]$: for these, as (6.3) shows, add up to 0.5, whereas $P_B[1]$, $P_B[3]$ and $P_B[5]$ must add up to 1.

The standard answer to this question assumes that B eliminates the points in $\underline{K}$ that are not in $\underline{B}$ (2, 4 and 6) without altering the *relative* probabilities of the points – 1, 3 and 5 – which remain. On this assumption, $P_B[1]$, $P_B[3]$ and $P_B[5]$ can be derived from $P[1]$, $P[3]$ and $P[5]$ by increasing the latters' values pro rata, which means dividing each of them by their *sum*, i.e. by B's prior probability $P(B)$. The effect in this case, given (6.2) and (6.3), is to make

(7.3) $P_B[1] = \dfrac{P[1]}{0.5} = 0.6; P_B[3] = \dfrac{P[3]}{0.5} = 0.2; P_B[5] = \dfrac{P[5]}{0.5} = 0.2.$

Note that this *pro rata rule* (as I shall call it) applies only to sample points and thus only to *simple* outcomes, like {1}, {3} and {5}, which contain only one point. It does not apply directly to *complex* outcomes, which contain two or more points. Assuming that B is true may not increase their prior probabilities pro rata, or even at all, because it may eliminate some or all of their original sample points, as it does for example from the complex outcomes {1,2,3} and {2,4,6}.

Nevertheless, the pro rata rule is enough to fix the posterior probabilities in $\underline{B}$ of *all* the outcomes in the original sample space $\underline{K}$. To see how, take any complex outcome $\underline{A}$. Its posterior probability $P_B(A)$ will be the sum of the posterior probabilities of all the sample points in $\underline{K}$ that are also in $\underline{A}$ and $\underline{B}$. But, given the pro rata rule, the posterior probabilities of these points will be their prior probabilities divided by $\underline{B}$'s prior probability $P(B)$. The sum of their posterior probabilities will therefore be the sum of their priors divided by $P(B)$. But the sum of the priors of all the points in $\underline{K}$ that are in both $\underline{A}$ and $\underline{B}$ is the prior probability, $P(A \wedge B)$, of the conjunction $A \wedge B$. So the pro rata rule makes the posterior probability $P_B(A)$ in $\underline{B}$ of any outcome $\underline{A}$ in $\underline{K}$

$$P_B(A) = \frac{P(A \wedge B)}{P(B)},$$

which by our definition (1.2) equals $P(A \mid B)$.

So whenever the pro rata rule applies, A's probability posterior to B will equal its prior probability conditional on B, on any interpretation of these probabilities. Thus suppose the probabilities in our die-throwing case are chances, read as frequencies in an actual or hypothetical sequence of throws. Then to assume B is to select the sub-sequence of throws with results 1, 3 or 5, a selection which, as the pro rata rule assumes, leaves unaltered the numbers, and hence the ratios of the relative frequencies, of throws with each of these three results.

Similarly, if these probabilities are credences, if accepting B as evidence raises our credence in B from a prior $CR(B)$, less than 1, to a posterior $CR_B(B) = 1$. If telling us that B is true is *all* this evidence does, it tells us nothing about which result of the throw – 1, 3 or 5 – actually made B true. In that case, accepting B should, as the pro rata rule assumes, leave the relative values of our credences in those three results unaltered. It should therefore only increase their old values pro rata, thus making our posterior credences in *any* outcome of the throw satisfy the subjective version of (1.2):

$$(7.4) \quad CR_B(A) = \frac{CR(A \wedge B)}{CR(B)} =_{df} CR(A \mid B);$$

where $CR(B)$ and $CR(A \wedge B)$ are our credences in B and in $A \wedge B$ before we learn that B is true. In words: our posterior *unconditional* credence in A after accepting evidence B should equal our prior *conditional* credence in A given B as defined by (1.2). That is why this way of updating our credences is called *conditionalisation*.

III

Epistemic Probabilities

Given the principle (EC) of 6.I, the pro rata rule also entails the epistemic reading,

$$(7.5) \quad \text{EP}(A \mid B \wedge K) = \frac{\text{EP}(A \wedge B \mid K)}{\text{EP}(B \mid K)},$$

of (1.2), where $\text{EP}(A \mid B \wedge K)$ measures the posterior credence we should have in A, given our new total evidence $B \wedge K$ and the prior credences which we should have had in B and in $A \wedge B$ given only our background evidence K.

To see how this way of deriving epistemic probabilities, by conditionalising credences on new evidence, lets evidence confirm some propositions and not others, consider the following outcomes in our die-throwing sample space $\underline{K}$:

$$\underline{A_1} = \{1,2\}, \quad \underline{A_2} = \{3,4\} \quad \text{and} \quad \underline{A_3} = \{5,6\};$$

as shown in Table 5.

Outcome A_i	A_1		A_2		A_3		Total
Points [j] in **K**:	1	2	3	4	5	6	6
In **K**: $P[j] =$	0.3	0.2	0.1	0.2	0.1	0.1	1
$P(A_i) =$	0.5		0.3		0.2		1
Points [j] in **B**:	1	–	3	–	5	–	3
In **K**: $P(A_i \wedge B) =$	0.3	–	0.1		0.1		0.5
In **B**: $P_B[j] = P[j]/P(B) =$	0.6	–	0.2	–	0.2	–	1
$P_B(A_i) = P(A_i \wedge B)/P(B) =$	0.6		0.2		0.2		1

Table 5

The table shows how, with the prior probabilities given in (7.1), the pro rata rule fixes the posterior probabilities in the new sample space B of the outcomes A_1, A_2 and A_3 and hence of the propositions A_1, A_2 and A_3. As the table shows, the rule makes changing the sample space from K to B affect these probabilities by

raising A_1's probability from 0.5 to 0.6,
lowering A_2's probability from 0.3 to 0.2, and
leaving A_3's probability unchanged at 0.2.

Thus, with an epistemic reading of the probabilities in Table 5, and given background evidence K, the evidence B, that the result of throwing the die is 1, 3 or 5,

confirms A_1, the hypothesis that the result was 1 or 2,
disconfirms A_2, the hypothesis that the result was 3 or 4, and
is *evidentially irrelevant* to A_3, the hypothesis that the result was 5 or 6.

So far so good for conditionalisation as a recipe for updating our credences in response to new evidence. The pro rata rule provides a credible if not conclusive case for that recipe. But that recipe alone cannot fully answer the question, raised at the end of chapter 6, of how to justify credences without postulating special confirmation relations. For as we have just noted in deriving (7.5), if

$$(7.4) \quad CR_B(A) = \frac{CR(A \wedge B)}{CR(B)} =_{df} CR(A \mid B)$$

is to be the posterior credence in A which our new evidence B justifies, then our prior credences $CR(A \wedge B)$ and $CR(B)$ must also be justified. This threatens a regress of justification which will be very familiar to philosophers from the theory of knowledge, a regress which must stop somewhere if conditionalisation is to justify any posterior credences at all. Where and how can we stop it, if we must?

IV

Problems with Priors

Can satisfying equation (7.4) really not justify a posterior credence $CR_B(A)$ unless the prior credences $CR(B)$ and $CR(A \wedge B)$ are also justified? Unfortunately, it seems not. Suppose for example that A says it will rain tonight and B says I am in the Sahara, and that if I come to believe B, my posterior $CR_B(A)$ will, as conditionalisation requires, equal my prior $CR(A \mid B)$. But this equality will only justify a posterior $CR_B(A)$ of, say, 0.8 if a prior $CR(A \mid B)$ of 0.8 is justified, which, given well-known facts about the Sahara, it is not. This need for prior justification becomes more obvious still as credences approach 1: for if I am not justified in thinking that if I *was* in the Sahara it *would* rain, that thought can hardly justify my thinking, when (I think) I *am* in the Sahara, that it *will* rain.

Conditionalisation's inability to create justification, as well as transmit it, is even clearer in equation

$$(7.5) \quad EP(A \mid B \wedge K) = \frac{EP(A \wedge B \mid K)}{EP(B \mid K)}.$$

For if $EP(A \wedge B \mid K)$ and $EP(B \mid K)$ fix $EP(A \mid B \wedge K)$ via (7.5), they too must be fixed, via

$$(7.6) \quad EP(A \wedge B \mid K) = \frac{EP(A \wedge B \wedge K)}{EP(K)} \text{ and}$$

$$(7.7) \quad EP(B \mid K) = \frac{EP(B \wedge K)}{EP(K)}$$

respectively, by EP$(A \wedge B \wedge K)$, EP$(B \wedge K)$ and EP(K). The problem is that these three probabilities are what I shall call *absolute* priors, i.e. conditional on no evidence at all, since all our evidence prior to B is, by definition, contained in our background evidence K. Yet how can an epistemic probability be conditional on *no* evidence?

This question has an easy formal answer. For even if EP$(A \wedge B \wedge K)$, EP$(B \wedge K)$ and EP(K) are not conditional on any *contingent* evidence, they can still be conditional on necessary truths. This is innocuous because, as we noted in chapter 6.IV, since necessary truths, such as those of logic and mathematics, are true in all possible worlds, they can tell us nothing about which world is actual, nor therefore about which contingent propositions are true in it. From this I inferred in chapter 6.IV that adding any necessary truth T to any contingent evidence for any contingent proposition A will not alter A's epistemic probability. Now, as a special case of that thesis, we may assume that adding T to *no* contingent evidence will also beg no evidential questions. This being so, we can always equate A's absolutely prior probability with EP$(A | T)$, A's epistemic probability given only necessary truths.

Unfortunately, the vacuity of necessary truths makes them as useless here as they are harmless, by stopping them giving absolute priors any definite values. What epistemic probability, for example, can the necessary truth that either it will rain or it will not give the proposition that it *will* rain? Hence the problem: for if the absolutely prior EP$(A \wedge B \wedge K)$, EP$(B \wedge K)$ and EP(K) lack values, (7.7) cannot give EP$(A \wedge B | K)$ and EP$(B | K)$ the values which (7.5) needs if it is to tell us how epistemically probable, given K, our evidence B makes the hypothesis A.

To all this we might reply that the absolute priors EP$(A \wedge B \wedge K)$, EP$(B \wedge K)$ and EP(K) are just trivial consequences of (7.5). They need not be *epistemically* prior in the sense of fixing A's epistemic probabilities given K and given B $\wedge$ K. The fixing might go the other way: our absolute priors might be fixed by the independently given values of EP$(A \wedge B | K)$ and EP$(B | K)$.

However, this reply will not work, for two reasons. First, we cannot derive *all* absolutely prior probabilities from posterior ones: we cannot for example use (7.7) to derive EP$(B \wedge K)$ from EP$(B | K)$ unless we already know the value of EP(K). And second, even if we could derive prior from posterior probabilities, what will fix the latters' values? It was after all our failure to answer that question in chapter 6 that is forcing us to look to (7.5) to answer it. But now it seems that we shall look in vain unless we can find a reading of prior probabilities which not only makes sense of them but lets them have values we can discover. Fortunately there is a reading which does just that: the subjective reading.

V

Prior Credences

We noted at the start of section IV that satisfying

$$(7.4) \quad \mathrm{CR}_B(A) = \frac{\mathrm{CR}(A \wedge B)}{\mathrm{CR}(B)} =_{df} \mathrm{CR}(A \mid B)$$

will only justify a posterior $\mathrm{CR}_B(A)$ if the prior $\mathrm{CR}(A \wedge B)$ and $\mathrm{CR}(B)$ are justified too, and what justifies them remains to be seen. But at least these priors make sense and have values we can know, since they are simply the credences in $A \wedge B$ and in B that we actually have before we learn that B is true. Thus if, to vary the example, A says that it will rain and B says that the atmospheric pressure is low, then $\mathrm{CR}(B)$ and $\mathrm{CR}(A \wedge B)$ are my credences, before I read my barometer, that the pressure is low and that it is both low and will be followed by rain.

This subjective reading also does not force us to know what our background evidence K is, since we need no such evidence to tell us how strongly we now believe B and $A \wedge B$. Nor therefore, given (7.4), need we know what K is in order to know our prior conditional credence $\mathrm{CR}(A \mid B)$. So we do not need subjective versions of (7.6) and (7.7) to derive our $\mathrm{CR}(A \mid B)$ from the absolutely prior credences that we would have if, *per impossibile*, we knew only necessary truths.

Suppose then that our actual prior credences $\mathrm{CR}(A \wedge B)$ and $\mathrm{CR}(B)$ *are* justified in some way that remains to be seen. If they are, then given conditionalisation, the posterior credence $\mathrm{CR}_B(A)$ given by (7.4) will also be justified. And to say this is, as we have seen, simply to say that $\mathrm{CR}(A \mid B)$, our prior conditional credence in A given B, is A's epistemic probability given B, i.e. that

$$(7.8) \quad \mathrm{EP}(A \mid B) = \mathrm{CR}(A \mid B) = \frac{\mathrm{CR}(A \wedge B)}{\mathrm{CR}(B)}.$$

For most and perhaps all contingent A and B, equation (7.8) offers the only way of ensuring that $\mathrm{EP}(A \mid B)$ exists and has a value that we can discover. This is why most advocates of conditionalisation, i.e. of the epistemic application of

$$(1.2) \quad \mathrm{P}(A \mid B) = \frac{\mathrm{P}(A \wedge B)}{\mathrm{P}(B)},$$

read the probabilities in (1.2) as credences and accept (7.8): for only then will the priors which an epistemic reading of (1.2) needs exist and be knowable.

VI

Bayes's Theorem

Since conditionalisation will only justify the posterior credences it generates, i.e. (7.8) will only be true, if the prior credences it uses are justified, its advocates need to say when they *are* justified. To see how that might be done, we turn now to perhaps the most well-known theorem of numerical probability, Bayes's Theorem. This theorem follows immediately from taking

(1.2) $\quad P(A \mid B) = \dfrac{P(A \wedge B)}{P(B)}$

to be true by definition (when $P(B) > 0$) for all A and B, and on all readings of probability. For then it must also be true by definition that, when $P(A) > 0$,

(7.9) $\quad P(B \mid A) = \dfrac{P(B \wedge A)}{P(A)}$.

And since, for all A and B and on all readings of probability, $P(B \wedge A) = P(A \wedge B)$, it follows that, if neither $P(A)$ nor $P(B)$ is zero,

(7.10) $\quad P(A \mid B) = \dfrac{P(B \mid A) \times P(A)}{P(B)}$.

This is the simple form of Bayes's Theorem.

Bayes's Theorem's evidential appeal lies in its derivation of $P(A \mid B)$, the probability of a hypothesis A given evidence B, from $P(B \mid A)$, the probability of B given A. This appeals especially if A is a statistical hypothesis which says that B has a specific chance $CH_A(B)$ of being true, for then (CE), the chances-as-evidence principle of chapter 6.IV, may tell us that

(7.11) $\quad EP(B \mid A) = CH_A(B)$.

Equation (7.11), by fixing the value of $P(B \mid A)$, reduces the problem of applying Bayes's Theorem epistemically to that of finding the prior epistemic probabilities $EP(A)$ and $EP(B)$. And in the special case where A is one of a number of hypotheses about $CH(B)$'s value, that problem can be reduced still further, as follows.

First we must note that as B is always logically equivalent to the disjunction $(B \wedge A) \vee (B \wedge \neg A)$ – since B can be true if and only if B is true and A is, or B is true and $\neg A$ is – their probabilities are always equal, so that

$P(B) = P[(B \wedge A) \vee (B \wedge \neg A)]$.

Moreover, since A and $\neg A$ are mutually exclusive – i.e. they cannot both be true – so too are $(B \wedge A)$ and $(B \wedge \neg A)$. Then applying the additivity principle of chapter 1.VIII, that

(1.12) $\quad$ If $A \wedge B$ is impossible, $P(A \vee B) = P(A) + P(B)$,

makes the probability of the disjunction $(B \wedge A) \vee (B \wedge \neg A)$, and hence that of B

(7.12) $P(B) = P(B \wedge A) + P(B \wedge \neg A)$.

Next we note that (7.9), which defines $P(B \mid A)$, B's conditional probability given A, and its analogue for $\neg A$, entail that

$$P(B \wedge A) = P(B \mid A) \times P(A) \text{ and}$$
$$P(B \wedge \neg A) = P(B \mid \neg A) \times P(\neg A).$$

We can therefore replace $P(B \wedge A)$ and $P(B \wedge \neg A)$ in (7.12) with $P(B \mid A) \times P(A)$ and $P(B \mid \neg A) \times P(\neg A)$ respectively to get

(7.13) $P(B) = P(B \mid A) \times P(A) + P(B \mid \neg A) \times P(\neg A)$.

This tells us that if we can use (7.11) to infer $P(B \mid A)$ from $CH_A(B)$, B's chance of being true if A is, and similarly for $P(B \mid \neg A)$, we can derive $P(B)$ from $P(A)$ and $P(\neg A)$ and hence – since $P(\neg A) = 1 - P(A)$ – from $P(A)$ alone. This will not always work, since A's being false may not entail that B has a definite chance, $CH_{\neg A}(B)$, of being true. But it will work if we know that B *does* have a chance, with n possible values given by n mutually exclusive hypotheses $A_1 \ldots A_n$. For in that case we can derive $P(B)$ from the more general form of (7.13),

(7.14) $P(B) = P(B \mid A_1) \times P(A_1) + \ldots + P(B \mid A_n) \times P(A_n)$,

which is standardly abbreviated to

(7.14) $P(B) = \sum_i P(B \mid A_i) \times P(A_i)$,

where i ranges from 1 to n. This, for each A_i, generates the more complex but often more useful form of Bayes's Theorem:

(7.15) $P(A_i \mid B) = \dfrac{P(B \mid A_i) \times P(A_i)}{\sum_i P(B \mid A_i) \times P(A_i)}$.

To see how (7.15) works in the simplest case, suppose we know, never mind how, that a fairly-tossed coin is either double-headed (A_1) or unbiased (A_2), i.e. that its chance of landing heads on any one toss is either 1 or 0.5. If these tosses are independent in the sense introduced in chapter 1.VII, the chance of getting two heads in a row is either 1 or $(1/2)^2 = 1/4$, of three heads in a row either 1 or $(1/2)^3 = 1/8$, and so on. Now suppose our evidence B is that two tosses both land heads. Then $CH_{A_1}(B)$, B's chance of being true if A_1 is true, is 1, and $CH_{A_2}(B)$, B's chance of being true if A_2 is true, $= 1/4$. These therefore, given (7.11), are the values of $EP(B \mid A_1)$ and $EP(B \mid A_2)$, B's epistemic probabilities given A_1 and A_2 respectively. Plugging these values into (7.15) for $i=2$ tells us that, given B, the epistemic probability of the coin being double-headed is

$$EP(A_1 \mid B) = \frac{1 \times EP(A_1)}{1/1 \times EP(A_1) + 1/4 \times EP(A_2)}.$$

And since we know that either A_1 or A_2 is true and hence that $EP(A_2) = 1 - EP(A_1)$, this means that

$$EP(A_1 \mid B) = \frac{EP(A_1)}{1/4 + 3/4 \times EP(A_1)},$$

which if $\text{EP}(A_1)$ is $1/2$, i.e. if before tossing the coin we were justified in thinking A_1 and A_2 equally likely, makes

$$\text{EP}(A_2 \mid B) = \frac{1/2}{1/4 + 3/4 \times 1/2} = 4/5.$$

This shows, as we might expect, that in these circumstances even two heads in a row strongly confirms the hypothesis that our coin is double-headed, by raising the epistemic probability of that hypothesis from $1/2$ to $4/5$.

VII

Bayesianism

We have seen how the complex form of Bayes's Theorem can be used to derive the epistemic probabilities of rival hypotheses, given suitable evidence B, from their prior probabilities plus B's epistemic probabilities given those hypotheses. This and related uses of the theorem have become so central to the practice of conditionalisation that advocates of this way of updating our credences are now generally called 'Bayesians' and their doctrines 'Bayesianism'.

The great advantage of Bayesian conditionalising, as our example shows, is its ability to make the prior probability of our evidence B a knowable function of the prior probabilities of the hypotheses about which B is our evidence. Their priors are all the input that (7.15) needs to fix the posterior probabilities which B gives them. And that in turn may be enough to tell us which of those hypotheses B confirms, regardless of their priors, provided these are not 0 or 1 (which would in any case make further evidence superfluous).

We can see all this, for our simple coin-tossing case, in Figure 4 below. This gives $\text{EP}(A_2 \mid B)$, the epistemic probability that our coin is double-headed, given two heads in a row, as a function of $\text{EP}(A_2)$, the prior probability of that hypothesis. As Figure 4 shows, $\text{EP}(A_2 \mid B) > \text{EP}(A_2)$ for all $\text{EP}(A_2)$ between 0 and 1, which tells us, not surprisingly, that whatever A_2's prior probability, the evidence B, of two heads in a row, confirms it.

None of this, however, solves the problem of priors, as Figure 4 also shows, and not only because we might want to know how *much* B raises A's probability: an amount which in Figure 4 ranges from 0.33 if $\text{EP}(A_2) = 0.3$ to 0.07 if $\text{EP}(A_2) = 09$. For what we really want B to tell us is not how much greater $\text{EP}(A_2 \mid B)$ is than $\text{EP}(A_2)$, but what its value is: i.e. how probable it is, given two heads in a row, that our coin is double-headed. And the answer to that question does depend greatly on $\text{EP}(A_2)$, as we can see from Figure 4, where it rises from 0.31 if $\text{EP}(A_2)$ is 0.1 to 0.97 if $\text{EP}(A_2)$ is 0.9.

In short, the problem of priors is still with us. Bayes's Theorem needs justified prior credences in order to justify the posterior credences that it makes evidence generate from them. Yet the theorem itself cannot tell us how to justify the prior credences it needs. Something else must do that: but what? In the next chapter we shall look at some possible candidates.

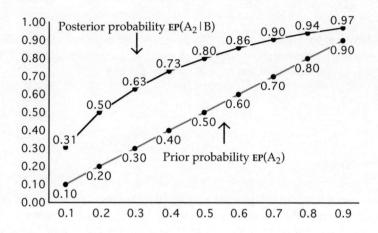

Figure 4: Prior and Posterior Probabilities

Further Reading

Swinburne (2002) contains a collection of articles on Bayes's Theorem and its applications, including Bayes's original (1763) paper. For a general defence of Bayesianism, see Howson and Urbach (1993). The primary sources for the so-called 'diachronic Dutch Book' argument for conditionalisation are Teller (1973) and Lewis (1997). Van Fraassen (1995) argues for a further constraint on rationality, which he calls 'reflection', and which invokes credences about one's own future credences. Christensen (1991), on the other hand, argues against the principle of reflection and the more persuasive justifications of conditionalisation.

8
Input Credences

I

Perception

The most obvious answer to the question of what justifies our prior credences is that they are justified by our perceptions. Thus in the coin-tossing case of chapter 7.VII, seeing that a coin is double-headed can both cause and justify a full belief – a credence at or very close to 1 – in the proposition A_2 that it *is* double-headed. However, to make this answer as useful as it is obvious, we must first remove an ambiguity in 'I see that A', 'I hear that A' etc., statements which may or may not be taken to entail that I fully believe the proposition A, and also that A is true. I shall take them to entail neither. That is, I shall assume that, when for example we see a conjuror pull a rabbit out of an empty hat, we need not believe what we see, and it need not be true.

This reading of 'see', 'hear', etc., and the generic 'perceive', will not beg any relevant questions. It simply lets us avoid having to say, in the conjuring case, that we only *seem* to see a rabbit emerge from an empty hat, a way of putting it that raises issues, about what it is to seem to see things, which do not matter here. What does matter here is that, in the present sense of 'see', seeing more or less clearly that a coin is double-headed can both cause and justify a credence in A_2 which may be less than 1, which this perception could not do if it entailed that the perceiver fully believed A_2 and that A_2 was true.

On this understanding of perceptions, they can easily cause credences that are prior in the sense of chapter 7.II. I may indeed need other beliefs about coins and what they look like before my seeing one can give me any degree of belief in A_2: my credence in A_2 may well be 'theory-laden' in that sense. But just as full beliefs which are theory-laden in that sense need not be inferred from less theory-laden beliefs, e.g. about the visual sensations I have when I see a coin, so theory-laden credences which are less than 1 need also not be derived, by conditionalisation or otherwise, from less theory-laden ones.

A credence in A_2 which is caused by a perception can therefore be what I shall call an *input* credence. For just as a full belief in a premise is an input to a process of inference, whose output is a full belief in its conclusion, so a Bayesian's prior credence is an input to a process of conditionalising, whose output is a posterior credence. And just as a chain of inferences, in order to justify its output, needs input beliefs that are justified in some other way, so conditionalising, to justify its output, needs input credences that are justified in some other way. So if it is no objection to theories of inference that they leave it to others to say when and how this need can be met, the same division of labour can be no objection to Bayesianism, especially as we know that in both cases the need can be met in the end by perception.

Perception is after all the ultimate source and justification of most if not all of our justified beliefs of whatever degree, at least in the contingent propositions that concern us, if not perhaps in the necessary propositions of mathematics and logic. This is so despite our being justified in believing many propositions that we have not ourselves perceived to be true but have only read or been told: i.e., beliefs whose proximate cause and justification is not perception but testimony. For testimony itself depends on perception, in at least two ways. First, we must perceive it: I must see what I am reading, or hear what I am being told, before it can cause me to believe anything. And second, as testimony is rarely if ever self-justifying, it too must derive ultimately from perception. Your telling me something will generally only cause me to believe it if I believe (a) that you believe it yourself and (b) that your belief is at least likely to be true. And for that to be so when what you tell me is contingent, your belief in it must be caused by perception; either directly, as when you tell me about something you yourself have seen, or indirectly, by inference or by more testimony, to which the same conditions will then apply.

It is, however, not enough to say that our input credences can be justified by being caused, directly or indirectly, by perceptions. We must say when and why credences so caused are thereby justified when credences caused in other ways are not. Take for example, by way of contrast, credences caused by wishful thinking. This is not always easy: no amount of it will, when I am soaked to the skin, make me believe to any finite degree that I am really dry. Yet wishful thinking does occur, when not flatly contradicted by our senses, as when we doubt bad news about ourselves that we would not doubt about others. And as for wishful thinking, so for the impact on our credences of other emotions, such as the jealousy which convinces Othello that Desdemona is unfaithful.

It is easy to see that credences caused in these ways are not thereby justified; it is harder to say why not and, more positively, to say not only how but when the credences that perception causes *are* justified. For the fact is that perceptions do not always justify the credences they cause. Suppose for example that I am deceived by a mirage, or that a barometer which persuades me that the atmospheric pressure is low is broken or miscalibrated. Are input credences caused by such misleading perceptions really justified? If not, we must say what it is that distinguishes credences which are justified by their perceptual causes from those which are not.

II

Consistency

The question of what justifies full beliefs is a familiar one in epistemology, and I shall assume that its various answers are well enough known not to need spelling out in detail here. All I think we need do here is see how one or two of them can be applied to input credences, and which of these might appeal to Bayesians.

I start with the so-called *coherence* or, as I shall call it, *consistency* theory, or rather theories: one of truth and another of justification. (I use 'consistency' to avoid confusion with coherence in the sense of chapter 5.III.) The consistency theory of truth says that our full beliefs *will* all be true if and only if they are all consistent with each other, meaning that all of them *could* be true. This theory, whose pros and cons will again be familiar to philosophers, is not one we need to consider here, except to remark that rules (1.13) to (1.20) of numerical probability, listed in chapter 1.VIII, make the theory at least logically tenable. For as we noted there, and as readers may easily verify, all these rules will continue to hold if we substitute 'A is true' for '$P(A) = 1$' and 'A is false' for '$P(A) = 0$'. This, reading these probabilities as credences, shows that if $CR(A) = 1$ is full belief in A and $CR(A) = 0$ is full belief in ¬A, then the logic of full belief can be the same as the logic of truth.

However, even if the consistency theory of truth is false, a consistency theory of justification might still be true. This theory says that our full beliefs are justified if and only if they are consistent. The theory cannot as it stands apply to most credences, because the truth or falsity of a proposition A cannot be ascribed to credences in A that differ much from 1. Suppose for example that my credence in A is 0.5 and thus equal to my credence in ¬A: in that case neither credence can be said to be either true or false, whether A is true or ¬A is.

What then is the analogue for credences of the consistency of full beliefs? To find out, we must recall that as I believe a proposition A more and more strongly, i.e. as my $CR(A)$ gets closer and closer to 1, it will eventually become a full belief in A. So a special case of the consistency requirement, namely that whenever we believe A we must disbelieve ¬A, entails that for all A,

(8.1) if $CR(A) = 1$, then $CR(¬A) = 0$.

(8.1) is not however an extra requirement which we need to impose on credences, since it follows from the rule (1.5), stated in chapter 1.VIII for probabilities of all kinds, that the probabilities of A and of ¬A must always add up to 1. This, for credences, means that, for all A,

(8.2) $CR(A) + CR(¬A) = 1$,

which in turn entails (8.1).

Perhaps then we can equate consistency in credences with their satisfying this and other basic rules of numerical probability. But that, for reasons given in chapter 5.III, we have already done. It is indeed debatable, as we saw in that chapter, whether our probability measure of belief is constitutive or merely normative, i.e. whether that measure *must* satisfy rules like (1.5) if it is to measure belief at all, or only that it would satisfy them if we were rational. But then the very same question arises about the consistency condition on full beliefs: does my fully believing A and B together show that B *cannot* be A's negation, or merely that I would be irrational if it were?

This, fortunately, is not a question we need to settle here, provided we give the same answer for credences and for full beliefs, in order to make (8.1) the special case of the consistency condition on full belief which it evidently is. On that understanding, we may assume that consistency requires credences to satisfy most if not all of the rules of numerical probability.

Note however that, so understood, consistency in credences, like consistency in full beliefs, is a static constraint, not a dynamic one. That is, it applies only to credences held by one person at one time. It does not require the credences I have today to be consistent with those I had yesterday, any more than it requires my credences to be consistent with yours. In particular, it does not require me to respond to new evidence by conditionalising on it, or indeed in any other specific way, provided my response makes my new credences consistent with each other. As a rule for updating our credences, conditionalisation must be argued for on other grounds, such as those given for the pro rata rule in chapter 7.II: it is not a requirement of consistency.

Conditionalisation however is not the issue here. The issue here is what justifies input credences and, specifically, whether consistency with all our other credences is enough to justify them. The naive case for taking consistency to be enough for justification – as for truth – is, basically, that it must be enough, since nothing else is available. We may want our input credences in contingent propositions to be justified (or made true) in some way by facts about the world, including, in the case of justification, facts about how reliable our senses are; but how can they be? We can have no access to facts about the world, including facts about the reliability of our senses, that is independent of our credences: all our information about the world that could tell us if and when our credences are justified (or true) must already be contained in those credences.

Consider for example the philosophical puzzle known as Moore's paradox: the absurdity of any thought or statement of the form 'A is true but I don't believe it'. This seems absurd because while it is true for many A – there are many truths we do not believe because we have never even thought of them – it seems all but impossible to believe. For if we believed any of our present beliefs to be false, we would not have those beliefs. The same goes for credences: I can hardly believe that my present credence in any A is too high or too low, for if I did I would have a different credence in A. So in particular I can hardly believe that any of my present input credences is too high – say because I believe it was caused by an unreliable perception, or by emotion or by wishful thinking – for if I did believe this, then that input credence would not *be* as high as it is.

These considerations are inconclusive, if only because, once we distinguish beliefs about our own beliefs from the beliefs they are about, we can see how it is possible, if unusual, to have a belief which we simultaneously believe to be false.

Instances of Moore's paradox may be rare and odd, but they need not be outright contradictions. Similarly, if I can have credences in my own present credences, I can have credences about which I am made uncertain by Freudian or other causes. There is no contradiction in having a credence $CR(A) = p$ together with a credence $CR(CR(A) = p)$ that is less than 1 and may even be close to 0.

However, none of this alters the fact that all we know, including all we know about our credences, is contained in our credences. This is why many Bayesians are so-called *internalists* in epistemology, since they believe that only credences can justify other credences. The main source of justification for them will be consistency, in the sense just spelled out, but it need not be the only one. They could for example also admit an internalised version of the chances-as-evidence principle (CE) of chapter 6.IV. In the simplest case, this would say that if all we *believe* about A or ¬A – or about their effects or their chances – is that $CH(A) = p$, then our $CR(A)$ should also be p. Similarly with any other 'external' criterion J of justification: it can always be internalised into the belief that J is satisfied. And if this can be done for credences in general, including input credences, then the question raised at the end of chapter 7, of how to justify our input credences, will need no external answer.

III

Reliability

It is, however, well known both that and how these and other arguments for consistency theories of truth or of justification may be resisted. The fact that our credences contain all we know about the world, including ourselves, does not rule out external sources of truth or justification. For even if we cannot always tell true from false beliefs in our present selves, we can always do so in our past selves and in other people. Similarly with justified and unjustified credences: criteria for telling them apart need not be statable only in first-person present-tense terms. It makes perfect sense to say, in impersonal and tenseless terms, that any person X's input credence $CR(A)$ is justified only if X and/or X's $CR(A)$ are related in some specific way to the outside world, and not just to X's other credences. Whether any such claim is true remains to be argued, but the idea is neither nonsensical nor incredible.

A Bayesian could admit then that input credences may need external as well as, or instead of, internal justification before output credences derived from them by conditionalisation are justified. They may deny that it is their job to say when input credences are justified, any more than it is a logician's job, when assessing an argument's deductive validity, to assess the truth or falsity of its premises. That, as we noted in section I, is a good point, and a fair division of epistemic labour. But that is all it is. It does not follow that conditionalisation can justify an output credence whether or not its input credences are justified, any more than a deduction can establish its conclusion whether or not its premises are true.

How then might credences be justified, if not just by consistency? Let us see, to give a definite example, how a so-called *reliabilist* theory of justified full belief can be extended to input credences. To do this, we need not give the theory in detail; a simple example will serve to show how, on such a theory, external facts about our senses can justify the full beliefs they cause.

Suppose then that proposition A says that a bird which I see flying past is a swallow, and suppose that I do not doubt my eyesight: the input $CR(A)$ it gives me will be either 1 or 0. Suppose also that, in the circumstances, my eyesight and birdwatching skills, such as they are, give me a chance p of getting $CR(A) = 1$ if A is true, and $CR(\neg A) = 1$ if A is false. Then in either case there will be a chance p that whichever belief I get, in A or in $\neg A$, will be true. Reliabilists may then say that when p reaches a certain value, say 0.95 or 0.99, my actual input credence, e.g. $CR(A) = 1$, will thereby be justified. (The minimum value of p may for example be fixed by how much it matters in the circumstances that whichever belief my senses give me should be true.)

To see how to extend this theory to credences less than 1, we may appeal first to an *un*internalised chances-as-evidence principle like (CE) to tell us when the evidence that A has a chance p should give us a credence p in A. We may then see why the fact that $CH(A)=p$ need not actually be part of our *evidence* about A for it to make p the right value, in the circumstances, of an input credence $CR(A)$.

To see this, consider insurance premiums, which are in effect what we pay for bets on whatever we are insuring against, e.g. the truth of the proposition A that I will catch an infectious disease D. This fact about insurance makes the ratio of my premium to the sum assured what in chapter 5.II I called the *cost/benefit* (or c/b) *ratio* of a bet on A. The highest value of this ratio that I will accept will then measure my credence in A under conditions, including those listed in 5.II, which seem to be met in this case. For it seems clear that the more strongly I believe that I will catch the disease D, i.e. the greater my $CR(A)$, the higher will be the highest premium that I will pay per unit of insurance against A: a premium which – unless I intend to defraud my insurers – we may therefore expect to equal my $CR(A)$.

Now suppose that, in the relevant circumstances, e.g. during an epidemic, my chance of catching D, $CH(A)$, is p. (CE) tells me that, if I know this, and not too much else, my credence in A, $CR(A)$, should also be p. But if $CH(A) = p$, then p is in fact the right c/b ratio for a bet on A, and hence, whether I know it or not, the right $CR(A)$ for me to have. So on a reliabilist view of justification, my $CR(A)$ can be justified by being caused by *non*-chance evidence that gives it a high enough chance, say 0.95 or 0.99, of being close enough to $CH(A)$, e.g. close enough to make me accept a premium per unit of insurance against A that is within, say, 0.05 of p.

What might this non-chance evidence be? The answer is that it is usually a frequency, which is after all what my insurers will use to calculate what we may call their *basic* premiums (i.e. what their premiums would be if they did not have to cover overheads and profits). Those premiums will be set by the fraction $f(D)$ of the relevant population to which I belong (e.g. unimmunised adult males) who catch the disease D. For as we shall see in chapter 10, if all members of this population have the same chance $CH(A)$ of catching D, the chance of $f(D)$ being close to $CH(A)$ increases rapidly with the size of the population. This means that, in a sufficiently large population, the policy of letting my $CR(A)$ equal $f(D)$ will give me a high enough chance of getting a $CR(A)$ which is close enough to $CH(A)$ for my purposes.

This is the analogue for credences of single perceptions giving the full beliefs they cause a chance of being true which is high enough for our purposes. So if perception can justify full beliefs by giving them a high enough chance of being true, then perceived frequencies can, by analogy, justify credences by giving them a high enough chance of being close enough to the corresponding chances. This is the natural extension to credences of a reliabilist theory of justified full belief.

Could Bayesians accept this sort of theory of justification for input credences? There are two reasons why they may not. One is that the initial credence caused by my observing the frequency $f(D)$ is a full belief in $f(D)$, which is what then causes my credence, $CR(A)$, that I will catch the disease D. But this makes my $CR(A)$ look more like an output credence than an input one. To this a reliabilist reply is that a $CR(A)$ caused in this way need no more be justified by conditional-isation than a $CR(A)$ that is caused by the evidence that $CH(A) = p$. In each case the $CR(A)$ is caused by a full belief via a rule – (CE) or its frequency analogue – which justifies it by giving it a high chance of being close to the external counterpart, $CH(A)$ or $f(D)$. A full belief that causes a $CR(A)$ in this way will indeed be justified, in the same reliabilist way, if the $CR(A)$ it causes is justified; but that is a side-effect. The full belief is not an input to a process of *conditional-isation* that has the $CR(A)$ which it causes as an output. So a $CR(A)$ justified in this reliabilist way can be a justified input credence to any ensuing conditionalisation.

The other Bayesian objection to reliabilism is that it postulates chances, which many Bayesians reject on ontological or epistemological grounds, as being either unintelligible (or at least unnecessary) or unknowable. They might, however, be willing to accept externalist theories which do not invoke chances. One such is Nozick's (1981b) 'tracking' theory of knowledge. If we equate my full belief in A with a credence in A that is close enough to 1, which I shall write '$CR(A) \approx 1$', this theory says that I know A if and only if

> A is true,
> my $CR(A) \approx 1$,
> if A were true then my $CR(A)$ would ≈ 1, and
> if A were not true then my $CR(A)$ would not ≈ 1.

This, in a traditional tripartite theory of knowledge as justified true belief, means that my $CR(A) \approx 1$ will be justified if and only if

(a) if A were true then my $CR(A)$ would ≈ 1, and
(b) if A were not true then my $CR(A)$ would not ≈ 1.

And as (a) and (b) include no chances, Bayesians could accept both of them and still insist that credence is the only kind of probability we need, at least in a theory of justification.

However, a problem arises in modifying (a) and (b) to extend Nozick's theory to all credences, the problem being that this extension seems to need chances. This is most obvious when $CR(A) \approx CR(\neg A) \approx 1/2$, since justifying roughly equal credences in A and in ¬A cannot require $CR(A)$'s values to depend on whether A is true or false. This being so, the only modification of (a) and (b) which might work seems to be something like

(a') if $CH(A)$ were close to p then my $CR(A)$ would be close to p, and
(b') if $CH(A)$ were not close to p then my $CR(A)$ would not be close to p.

But even this will not do, and not only because it postulates chances. It will not do because if we know what $CH(A)$ is, we need neither (a') nor (b'), since they both follow from (CE). While if we do not know $CH(A)$, and rely on frequency evidence instead, then neither (a') nor (b') is available: for the most that could be guaranteed by the causal link discussed above, between perceived frequencies and credences, is that, for all p,

if $CH(A) = p$ then my $CR(A)$ has a high *chance* of being close to p,

which entails neither (a') nor (b'). In short, extending Nozick's theory to cover all credences either makes it useless or reduces it to reliabilism.

The fate of Nozick's theory illustrates how hard it is for externalist theories of justification for credences to avoid postulating chances. Yet, oddly enough, Bayesians who reject chances could still accept externalism, at least in its letter, if not in its spirit. For as we shall see in chapter 10, there are subjective surrogates for chances, which those who reject chances use to explain away the apparent links between chances and frequencies that reliabilists and others exploit. How well these surrogates work remains to be seen; but if they work at all, they can certainly cope with any chances that may be needed to give input credences an external justification. And if they can cope with those chances, then subjectivist Bayesians can easily accept any form of externalism for the time being, pending its reduction to what at the end of section II I called an 'internalised' version of it.

Finally, however, we should note that although many Bayesians do reject chances, nothing in their core doctrine of conditionalisation forces them to do so. So whether or not a subjective surrogate for chance succeeds, a commitment to upgrading credences by conditionalisation is consistent with any independently viable theory of what justifies the input credences which that upgrading needs.

IV

Uncertain Evidence

So far in this chapter, in considering how to use equation

$$(7.4) \quad CR_B(A) = \frac{CR(A \wedge B)}{CR(B)} =_{\mathrm{df}} CR(A \mid B)$$

to justify a posterior credence $CR_B(A)$, we have concentrated on how to justify the prior credences $CR(B)$ and $CR(A \wedge B)$. The new evidence B, which is what makes us update our credence in A to $CR_B(A)$, we have so far taken for granted in two ways. First, we have assumed that, however we acquire the evidence B, the way we do so justifies us in believing B, i.e. in raising our credence in B from its prior $CR(B)$ to a posterior $CR_B(B) = 1$. For if it did not, (7.4) would no more justify our posterior $CR'(A)$ than it would if our prior $CR(B)$ and $CR(A \wedge B)$ were unjustified.

The discussion in sections II and III, of how to justify input credences, applies therefore as much to $CR_B(B) = 1$, our posterior belief in B, as to $CR(B)$, our prior credence in B. In particular, we may take this evidential input to be justified, directly or indirectly, by perception. Which brings us to our other tacit assumption about acquiring evidence B, namely that it always gives us full belief in B, by raising our credence in B to 1. In other words, we assume that our evidence B is always certain, or rather that we are always certain of it. Yet that seems to be neither true nor necessary. It seems not to be true given the betting measure of belief introduced in chapter 5.II, on which a credence of 1 – as opposed to 0.999... – in any proposition B implies a willingness to risk infinite loss if B is false for a penny gain if it is true. How often are we, or should we be, that sure of what we see or hear? Nor is it necessary for us to be that sure, now we have seen in the last two sections how perceptions can cause and justify input credences less than 1. If they can do this for a prior $CR(B)$, they can do it for a posterior credence in B which is less than 1, since that is as much an input to the process of conditionalisation as $CR(B)$ is.

Bayesians should therefore be able to cope with input credences in B that are less than 1. This however is not easily done, because the assumption that our evidence B is certain (in this subjective sense) is built into the equation (7.4) that Bayesians use to fix our posterior credence in A on acquiring this evidence. It is also, more trivially, built into our symbolism, since writing an input credence in B as '$CR_B(B)$' makes it look necessary that its value is 1. But if evidence can be uncertain, it can make this credence less, not only than 1 but than a prior $CR(B)$, in which case it *reduces* our credence in B, or even than 1/2, in which case the evidence is ¬B rather than B. To express all this, I shall now write '$CR_{\pm B}(B)$' for any input credence in B that may be less than 1, and reserve '$CR_B(B)$' for evidence that is assumed to be *certain*; and similarly for the resulting output credences in A, $A \wedge B$, etc.

Because generalising the basic concept of conditionalisation to cover uncertain evidence is especially complex when several credences are input at once, I shall only present the simplest case where only our credence in B is changed, from a prior $CR(B)$ to a higher posterior $CR_{+B}(B)$.

To do this, we must start by recalling from chapter 7.VI that for all A and B, and on all interpretations of probability,

(7.13) $\quad P(B) = P(B \mid A) \times P(A) + P(B \mid \neg A) \times P(\neg A).$

This, if we exchange 'A' and 'B' and then replace '$P(\neg B)$' with '$1 - P(B)$', gives us

(8.3) $\quad P(A) = P(A \mid B) \times P(B) + P(A \mid \neg B) \times [1 - P(B)].$

A subjective reading of the probabilities in (8.3) then entails

$$(8.4) \quad CR(A) = CR(A \mid B) \times CR(B) + CR(A \mid \neg B) \times [1 - CR(B)]$$

for our *prior* credences, and

$$(8.5) \quad CR_{\pm B}(A) = CR_{\pm B}(A \mid B) \times CR_{\pm B}(B) + CR_{\pm B}(A \mid \neg B) \times [1 - CR_{\pm B}(B)]$$

for our *posterior* ones, i.e. for those we have after our uncertain evidence B has changed our credence in B from $CR(B)$ to $CR_{\pm B}(B)$.

Now suppose there is such an input change in $CR(B)$, and that $CR_{\pm B}(A)$ is an *output* credence, i.e. one that suffers no simultaneous input change. If the input $CR_{\pm B}(B) = 1$, equation (7.4) above prescribes a posterior $CR_{\pm B}(A) = CR(A \mid B)$, a prescription which assumes that this increase in $CR(B)$ will not change $CR(A \mid B)$, our prior conditional credence in A given B. This assumption is usually quite credible, as two examples may suffice to show. My prior credence in rain tonight, conditional on the atmospheric pressure being low, will not be altered by my learning that the pressure *is* low; and my prior credence in your getting cancer, conditional on your smoking, will not be altered if I then learn that you *do* smoke.

Similarly when our evidence is not B but $\neg B$, and is also certain, i.e. makes $CR_{\pm B}(\neg B) = 1$ and therefore $CR_{\pm B}(B) = 0$. Now equation (7.4), with 'B' replaced by '$\neg B$', prescribes a $CR_{\pm B}(A) = CR(A \mid \neg B)$, which should therefore also not be altered by this input change in $CR(B)$. That too seems right: seeing my barometer read 'high' will not alter my prior credence in rain conditional on that reading; nor will my prior credence in your getting cancer, conditional on the proposition that you do *not* smoke, be altered by my learning that you do indeed not smoke.

And as for input changes in $CR(B)$ which make it 0 or 1, so, we shall now assume, for *all* input changes in $CR(B)$: *no* such change will alter either $CR(A \mid B)$ or $CR(A \mid \neg B)$. Thus suppose for example that I take my barometer's readings with a pinch of salt: with a 'low' reading only raising my credence in the proposition B that the pressure is low from (say) 0.4 to 0.9, and a 'high' reading lowering it only to 0.1. Neither of these changes, we are now assuming, will affect either $CR(A \mid B)$ or $CR(A \mid \neg B)$, my prior credences in rain conditional on B and on $\neg B$ respectively; and similarly for all other cases of uncertain evidence.

This assumption entails that, for all contingent hypotheses A and evidence B, and all input changes in $CR(B)$,

$$CR_{\pm B}(A \mid B) = CR(A \mid B) \text{ and } CR_{\pm B}(A \mid \neg B) = CR(A \mid \neg B).$$

This lets us replace '$CR_{\pm B}(A \mid B)$' and '$CR_{\pm B}(A \mid \neg B)$' in (8.5) by their prior counterparts, to get the prescription that

$$(8.6) \quad CR_{\pm B}(A) = CR(A \mid B) \times CR_{\pm B}(B) + CR(A \mid \neg B) \times [1 - CR_{\pm B}(B)],$$

an equation which makes the difference between $CR_{\pm B}(A)$ and

$$(8.4) \quad CR(A) = CR(A \mid B) \times CR(B) + CR(A \mid \neg B) \times [1 - CR(B)]$$

depend *only* on the input change in our credence in B from $CR(B)$ to $CR_{\pm B}(B)$.

Prescription (8.6) is the one we need, since it tells us how *any* input change in a non-zero prior $CR(B)$ should determine the value of the output credence $CR_{\pm B}(A)$.

In so doing, it shows how, in a simple case, conditionalisation can be extended to cover uncertain as well as certain evidence. This extension is not a rival to basic Bayesianism, nor a variant of it, merely a generalisation to cases which the basic doctrine does not cover: as is shown by the fact that when $CR_{+B}(B) = 1 = CR_B(B)$, equation (8.6) reduces to the original Bayesian

(7.4) $CR_B(A) = CR(A \mid B)$.

This way of enabling Bayesians to cope with uncertain evidence is very attractive, but it does have features that make it more contentious than the basic Bayesian recipe. One is that the order in which we acquire two or more pieces of uncertain evidence about a proposition A can affect our final output credence in A. Still, while this result is undeniably unexpected, it is also not so clearly wrong as to rule out this way of conditionalising; and so I shall not demonstrate or discuss it further. A more serious reason for Bayesians to jib at this generalisation of their theory is that, as we shall see, accepting it undermines the rationale for conditionalising even on evidence which is certain. This therefore is a factor that must be included in the overall assessment of Bayesianism, to which we now turn.

Further Reading

The above sketch of how to generalise conditionalisation to cope with uncertain evidence is derived from chapter 11 of Jeffrey (1983). Sections 6–8 of that chapter show how, on this theory, our output credence in A can depend on which of two or more pieces of uncertain evidence we acquire first.

For the coherence theory of truth, see Kirkham (1998) or Walker (1989). For Moore's paradox, see Baldwin (1990), chapter VII, section 5. Lehrer (1974) defends a coherence theory of justification, and Armstrong (1973) a reliabilist one.

For criticisms of Nozick's 'tracking' theory of knowledge, see Luper-Foy (1987) and for a comprehensive and readable introduction to internalist and externalist theories of knowledge, justification and perception, see Dancy (1985). Dancy (1988) contains a good selection of papers, including work on externalist theories of knowledge and perceptual knowledge by Nozick (1981a), Goldman (1976), Grice (1961) and Lewis (1980b).

9

Questions for Bayesians

I

Sample Spaces

In chapter 7.II an argument was given for the so-called pro rata rule, and hence for conditionalisation. The argument equates all conditional probabilities given any proposition B with those in a sample space $\underline{B}$ derived from a prior space $\underline{K}$ by eliminating all the points in $\underline{K}$ which are not in $\underline{B}$. In the example used to illustrate this argument, $\underline{K}$ is the set $\{1,2,3,4,5,6\}$ of possible results of throwing a die, and $\underline{B}$ is the subset, $\{1,3,5\}$, of the points in $\underline{K}$ which make true the proposition B that the result of the throw is an odd number.

On a subjective reading of these probabilities, this sample space argument assumes that acquiring evidence B always reduces to zero our credence in all the sample points in $\underline{K}$ which are not in $\underline{B}$. This assumption, by making our credence in ¬B zero, entails that our input credence in B, CR′(B), will always be 1. In other words, the argument assumes that our evidence is always *certain*, in the sense that we always fully believe it.

Now however, in chapter 8.IV, we have seen how conditionalisation can be extended to cover evidence B which is *uncertain*, i.e. where our input credence in B is less than 1. Can we extend the sample space argument for conditionalisation in the same way? It is not obvious that we can, since our credence in B can only be less than 1 if our credence in ¬B is greater than zero. But for that to be so, some at least of the sample points which B excludes must have – and all of them may have – a non-zero probability.

Thus suppose in our example that, because I doubt the reliability of whomever tells me that B is true – i.e. that the throw of the die produced an odd number – this information raises my prior credence in B not to 1 but only to (say) 0.85. The information therefore cannot reduce to zero *all* my credences in the results 2, 4 and 6 which B excludes, since these credences must now add up to 0.15. Indeed it may not reduce *any* of them to zero, since it might, for example, leave them all equal, so that

$$\text{CR}_{\pm B}[2] = \text{CR}_{\pm B}[4] = \text{CR}_{\pm B}[6] = 0.05.$$

It follows then that, when evidence B is uncertain, it cannot remove from our old sample space $\underline{K}$ all the points that are not in $\underline{B}$, and it may not remove any of them. So in order to extend to uncertain evidence the sample space argument for conditionalisation, we must represent B in a way which does not require it to eliminate points from $\underline{K}$. Fortunately this is easily done, as evidence need *never* eliminate sample points. For even when it reduces our credences in some sample points to zero, as it must when we are certain of it, and may when we are not, we need not *remove* those points from $\underline{K}$: since nothing prevents a sample point having zero probability.

However, this way of coping with uncertain evidence presents a problem: we can no longer use the pro rata rule to justify conditionalisation. The reason is that unless our evidence B reduces the probabilities of all the sample points it rules out to zero, we cannot assume that the probabilities of all the other points in K increase pro rata. For if our evidence B leaves us with a non-zero credence in ¬B, it does *not* rule out all the sample points that are not in $\underline{B}$: it leaves some of them with non-zero probabilities, some of which our evidence must *decrease* if it is to raise our credence in B itself. But if our evidence does not increase pro rata the probabilities of all the points that it does not rule out, why should it increase any of them pro rata? The reason can no longer be, as the pro rata rule assumes, that our evidence never changes our relative credences in the sample points it does not rule out, since evidence which is uncertain does just that.

Bayesians may therefore reject the whole idea of uncertain evidence, because of the threat it poses to the pro rata rule. This indeed is partly why the generalised conditionalisation of 8.IV, designed precisely to accommodate such evidence, is more contentious than its basic counterpart, which the pro rata rule can justify. Yet this tactical retreat may not work, for two reasons. One is that the existence of uncertain evidence is hard to deny, given that, as we noted in chapter 8.IV,

> a credence of 1 . . . in any proposition B implies a willingness to risk infinite loss if B is false for a penny gain if it is true. How often are we, or should we be, that sure of what we see or hear?

So denying uncertain evidence may mean denying that much of what we *call* evidence *is* evidence, or at least evidence that can justify conditionalisation.

The other reason for admitting that evidence can be uncertain is that denying it may still not save the pro rata rule. For if evidence that is uncertain will change our relative credences in some sample points which it does not rule out, how can we be sure that even evidence that is certain will never do so? Take for example the following variant of our die-throwing case.

Suppose I am justified in believing that a die is fair and will be fairly thrown. This justifies me in having equal prior credences of 1/6 in all the possible results, 1, 2, 3, 4, 5 and 6, of the throw. Now suppose that, after the throw, I see that it landed 4, 5 or 6: this is my evidence B, and I am certain of it. For while I am too short-sighted to see exactly how many black spots the top face of the die has, it looks black enough to convince me that it has more than three, thus raising my credence in B to 1. But the die's top face also looks black enough to raise my credence in 6 more than my credences in 5 and in 4. So although my perception reduces my credence in ¬B to zero, it does not (and seemingly should not) raise my prior credences of 1/6 in the three surviving sample points pro rata, i.e. in this case by the same amount. Yet that is what the pro rata rule, and therefore conditionalisation, says it should do.

Here then is a situation to which the pro rata rule applies, but where the conditionalisation that it entails seems wrong; and what is wrong in this case may be wrong in other cases too. In particular, it seems that even evidence of which we are certain may change our relative credences in some of the sample points which it does not rule out. Yet if the pro rata rule is not self-evidently right whenever it applies, it may no more justify conditionalising on evidence that is certain than on evidence that is not. For a general justification of conditional-isation, if there is one, we shall have to look elsewhere, starting with a promising proposition from Bayes's (1763) paper.

II

Bayes's Proposition 3

Proposition 3 of Bayes's paper says that

> The probability that two subsequent events will both happen is a ratio compounded of the probability of the 1st, and the probability of the 2nd on the supposition that the 1st happens.

If we read 'probability' here as chance, we may illustrate this proposition with a coin-tossing example. Let B say that a coin is tossed and A say that it lands heads. Now suppose it is a matter of chance whether B is true, perhaps because the coin will be tossed if and only if another coin toss lands heads. Then there is, *before* our coin is tossed, what we may therefore call a *prior* chance $\mathrm{CH}(B)$ that it will be tossed. Finally, suppose that *if* the coin is tossed, it will have a certain chance of landing heads, a chance which, to avoid begging present questions, I shall follow the notation of chapter 7.VI and write not as '$\mathrm{CH}(A \mid B)$' but as '$\mathrm{CH}_B(A)$'. What then is the value of $\mathrm{CH}(A \wedge B)$, the chance, prior to the toss, of the conjunction $A \wedge B$, that the toss will take place and will land heads, being true?

To this question Bayes's answer, in our symbols, is that $\mathrm{CH}(A \wedge B)$ is the product of $\mathrm{CH}_B(A)$ and $\mathrm{CH}(B)$, i.e. that

$$\mathrm{CH}(A \wedge B) = \mathrm{CH}_B(A) \times \mathrm{CH}(B).$$

From this, provided that $\mathrm{CH}(B)$, our coin's prior chance of being tossed, is greater than zero, it follows at once that

$$\mathrm{CH}_B(A) = \frac{\mathrm{CH}(A \wedge B)}{\mathrm{CH}(B)}.$$

This in turn, given our general definition of conditional probability, entails that

$$(9.1) \quad \text{CH}_B(A) = \frac{\text{CH}(A \wedge B)}{\text{CH}(B)} =_{df} \text{CH}(A \mid B).$$

Equation (9.1) is similar in form to the simple Bayesian rule for evidence B which is certain, i.e. which generates an input credence $\text{CR}_B(B) = 1$:

$$(7.4) \quad \text{CR}_B(A) = \frac{\text{CR}(A \wedge B)}{\text{CR}(B)} =_{df} \text{CR}(A \mid B).$$

But (9.1) differs from (7.4) in two key ways. First, it relates chances rather than credences. Second, given $\text{CH}(B)$, it is the value of $\text{CH}_B(A)$ which fixes the value of $\text{CH}(A \wedge B)$ and thereby of $\text{CH}(A \mid B)$, not the other way round, as with the corresponding credences of (7.4). Given these differences, how can Bayes's proposition 3, interpreted as equation (9.1), bear on Bayesianism?

To see how, suppose first that I know the values of $\text{CH}(B)$, the coin's chance of being tossed, and $\text{CH}(A \wedge B)$, its chance of being tossed and landing heads. Then our chances-as-evidence principle (CE) may tell us that these should also be the values of my prior credences, before the toss, in those two propositions:

$$(9.2) \quad \text{CR}(B) = \text{CH}(B); \text{CR}(A \wedge B) = \text{CH}(A \wedge B).$$

Now suppose that I also know the value of $\text{CH}_B(A)$, i.e. what the coin's chance of landing heads will be *if* it is tossed. It is a very plausible extension of (CE) to take this to be the value of the credence which I should have in A if and when I learn that the coin *is* tossed, i.e. the posterior credence $\text{CR}_B(A)$ of (7.4), so that

$$(9.3) \quad \text{CR}_B(A) = \text{CH}_B(A).$$

Then if the chances $\text{CH}(B)$, $\text{CH}(A \wedge B)$ and $\text{CH}_B(A)$ satisfy (9.2) and (9.3), it follows at once that the corresponding credences, $\text{CR}(A \wedge B)$, $\text{CR}(B)$ and $\text{CR}_B(A)$ will satisfy (7.4), as basic Bayesianism requires.

This result does not, however, entitle us to read (7.4) as the Bayesian rule for updating our prior credence in A by conditionalising on new evidence B. For in (9.3), $\text{CR}_B(A)$, our prescribed posterior credence in A given evidence B, is derived directly from the corresponding chance $\text{CH}_B(A)$, A's chance of being true if B is. It is not derived from any prior credence, not even from $\text{CR}(A \wedge B)$ and $\text{CR}(B)$, and certainly not from $\text{CR}(A)$, our prior credence in A, about which Bayes's proposition 3 assumes nothing at all.

Bayes's proposition 3 therefore offers no logical support to Bayesianism, even when the relevant chances exist and are known, let alone when they are not. But it does offer Bayesianism some psychological support. For as we noted in chapter 5.I, it is often tempting to identify a credence $\text{CR}(A) = p$ in a proposition A with the full belief that, in some objective sense, A has a chance p of being true, i.e. with the credence $\text{CR}(\text{CH}(A)=p) = 1$. This identification then makes it equally tempting to read (9.2) and (9.3) as deriving chances from credences, rather than the other way round, and hence as telling us, via Bayes's proposition 3, that our posterior credence in A given B should be related to our prior credences in B and $B \wedge A$ by (7.4), i.e. by conditionalisation.

III

Decisions and Credences

Another problem arises for Bayesianism when we try to apply it to the decision theory outlined in chapter 5.V. Bayesianism says that $CR_B(A)$, the output credence in A which an input credence $CR(B) = 1$ would cause, should satisfy

$$(7.4) \quad CR_B(A) = \frac{CR(A \wedge B)}{CR(B)} =_{df} CR(A \mid B).$$

This prescription assumes that, before we learn that B is true, we have a non-zero credence in B and a credence (which may be zero) in $A \wedge B$. Yet in the key stages of decision-making which rely on $CR_B(A)$, we need have no such prior credences. How then can (7.4) tell us what our $CR_B(A)$, and hence our decision, should be?

Suppose, to revisit an example from 5.V, B says that I stop smoking and A says that I avoid getting cancer. I am trying to decide whether to make B true, a decision which, on the decision theory of 5.V, will depend on whether $ESU(B)$, the expected subjective utility for me of a smoke-free future, is greater or less than $ESU(\neg B)$. The values of these two expected utilities are given by

$$(5.3) \quad ESU(B) = [CR_B(A) \times SU(B \wedge A)] + [CR_B(\neg A) \times SU(B \wedge \neg A)]$$

and its counterpart for $ESU(\neg B)$, where $SU(B \wedge A)$ is the actual subjective utility for me of $B \wedge A$, and similarly for the three other possible outcomes of my decision.

As (5.3) shows, $ESU(B)$ depends on $CR_B(A)$, the credence I would have in A if I fully believed B, and similarly for $ESU(\neg B)$. So whether I *should* make B true also depends on what my $CR_B(A)$ should be, which for Bayesians is fixed, via (7.4), by my prior $CR(A \wedge B)$ and $CR(B)$. The problem is that while trying to decide whether to make B true, I may well have no idea what my decision will be, and therefore no credence at all, high or low, in B and hence none in $A \wedge B$. But when $CR(A \wedge B)$ and $CR(B)$ have no value, neither does $CR(A \wedge B)/CR(B)$, to which (7.4) says my $CR_B(A)$ should be equal. So when I am trying to decide how to act, Bayesianism may well be unable to say what I should think and therefore what I should do.

The same problem can also arise, for a different reason, after I have made my decision. Suppose I decide to go on smoking ($\neg B$) because $ESU(\neg B)$, the expected subjective utility for me of doing so, is greater than $ESU(B)$. This decision of mine, to make B false, will certainly make my credence in B very low, and arguably zero. So now suppose that, without wavering in my resolve, I reconsider its decision-theoretic rationale by using (5.3) to recalculate $ESU(B)$. But if $CR(B)$, my credence in B, and hence $CR(A \wedge B)$, my credence in B's conjunction with A, are both zero, then

$$\frac{CR(A \wedge B)}{CR(B)} = \frac{0}{0}$$

is undefined. Here too (7.4) can say nothing about what my $CR_B(A)$ should be – except perhaps that it too should be undefined, which is absurd.

Note by the way that we cannot solve either of these problems by taking the conditional probability $P(A \mid B)$ to be a primitive notion, to be given the value of $P(A \wedge B)/P(B)$ only when that fraction is defined and has a value. The problem that arises when $CR(A \wedge B)/CR(B)$ lacks a value is not that $CR(A \mid B)$ does not exist, or is not defined, but that its value cannot then be determined by that of $CR(A \wedge B)/CR(B)$.

At this point we could perhaps try giving my $CR_B(A)$ the value, p say, which my $CR(A \wedge B)/CR(B)$ *would* have *if* I had a definite non-zero credence in B. In other words, in the symbolism introduced in chapter 8.IV to express uncertain evidence, we could say that for all non-zero input credences in B,

(9.4) $CR_{\pm B}(A \wedge B) = p \times CR_{\pm B}(B),$

where p is a constant.

This, however, only raises two further questions. First, what then justifies the assumption in (9.4) that $CR(A \wedge B)/CR(B)$ would have the same value p for all non-zero values of $CR(B)$? Second, if (9.4) *is* true for some p, it will be made true by the value of a conditional credence, $CR_{\pm B}(A \wedge B)$, which for Bayesians should itself be fixed by the generalised conditionalisation of 8.IV, in this case by

(9.5) $CR_{\pm B}(A \wedge B) = CR(A \wedge B \mid B) \times CR_{\pm B}(B) + CR(A \wedge B \mid \neg B) \times [1 - CR_{\pm B}(B)].$

And since, on all readings of probability, given non-zero $P(B)$ and $P(\neg B)$,

$$P(A \wedge B \mid B) = \frac{P(A \wedge B \wedge B)}{P(B)} = \frac{P(A \wedge B)}{P(B)}, \text{ and}$$

$$P(A \wedge B \mid \neg B) = \frac{P(A \wedge B \wedge \neg B)}{P(\neg B)} = \frac{0}{P(\neg B)} = 0,$$

(9.5) reduces to

(9.6) $CR_{\pm B}(A \wedge B) = \dfrac{CR(A \wedge B)}{CR(B)} \times CR_{\pm B}(B).$

This means that, to satisfy (9.4), Bayesians need to show that

(9.7) $\dfrac{CR(A \wedge B)}{CR(B)} = p,$

where $CR(A \wedge B)$ and $CR(B)$ are my *actual* credences in $A \wedge B$ and in B prior to my hypothetical non-zero input credence in B. But since by hypothesis these prior credences of mine either have no value or are zero, (9.7) cannot be true, and we are no further forward. When, because $CR(A \wedge B)/CR(B)$ has no value, we cannot use (7.4) to say what $CR_B(A)$ should be, we can also, and for the same reason, not use (9.6) to say what $CR_{\pm B}(A \wedge B)$ should be.

What then, if not my present credences in B and in $A \wedge B$, fixes the value p of $CR_B(A)$ that our decision theory uses to say what makes me decide to make B false? Something must do so if that decision is to make causal sense: my decision to make B false cannot depend causally on the non-existent credence in A that I would have had if I had fully believed B, which by hypothesis I do not. On what present surrogate for that credence might this decision then depend?

One possibility is a present *disposition* to have a credence p in A if I believed B, a disposition with which my $CR_B(A)$ can then be identified. This, however, needs the *realist* view of dispositions discussed in chapter 4.III, to enable my $CR_B(A)$ to be a cause of my decision. And while this view of dispositions is now widely held – partly because it does let them be causes – it may still be too contentious to be taken for granted here.

The other possible surrogate for the non-existent $CR(A)$ that I would have if I believed B is my present full belief that, if I did believe B, my $CR(A)$ would be p. This belief need not be true, since $CR(CR_B(A)=p) = 1$ does not entail $CH_B(A)=p$, and indeed it may not be true, since learning that B is true might give me a different $CR(A)$. But this is beside the point, as it is that, on a realist view, a dispositional $CR_B(A)$ might fail in the same way, since coming to believe B might change that disposition. What matters here is that a $CR(CR_B(A)=p) = 1$, like a real dispositional $CR_B(A)=p$, is a present state of mind on which a present decision to make B false – or to make it true – can causally depend.

This second way of saying how our decisions might be caused, by replacing $CR_B(A) = p$ with $CR(CR_B(A)=p) = 1$, looks like the temptation, noted at the end of section II, to identify a credence $CR(A) = p$ with $CR(CH(A)=p) = 1$. Here however, we may safely yield to this temptation, since it neither postulates a belief in a $CH(A)$ that we may not have, or be entitled to, nor confuses my $CR_B(A) = p$ with a belief in it which, if I can tell what I am thinking, I can certainly have and be entitled to.

One question remains, on both the options we have canvassed. What should be the value of p in $CR(CR_B(A)=p) = 1$, or a dispositional $CR_B(A) = p$? The answer is easy if A has a chance $CH_B(A)$ of being true if B is, and we know what this chance is. For then our chances-as-evidence principle (CE), as extended in section II, tells us that p should equal $CH_B(A)$. And even if we know of no such chance, we may still, as we have just noted, be tempted to think that we do, by equating our credence in A with the full belief that A has a corresponding chance. Here, moreover, the temptation may be particularly strong, especially if what drives our decision-making is a full belief that $CR_B(A)=p$, a belief that is easily misread as the full belief that $CH_B(A)$, A's *chance* of being true if B is, is p.

Here however, unlike section II, this temptation to mistake credences for full beliefs in chances offers no support to Bayesianism. It may still tempt us to read

$$(9.3) \quad CR_B(A) = CH_B(A)$$

as deriving a justified belief in $CH_B(A)$ from a justified $CR_B(A)$. But this derivation only regenerates our original question of how

$$(7.4) \quad CR_B(A) = \frac{CR(A \wedge B)}{CR(B)} =_{df} CR(A \mid B)$$

can justify $CR_B(A)$ when $CR(B)$ has no non-zero value, a question to which we have found no Bayesian answer. Moreover, if one of the non-Bayesian answers we have found is right when (7.4) is not available, why should that answer not also be right when it is available? If, in our earlier example, my decision to carry on smoking (¬B) cannot be justified by (7.4) when I have no non-zero $CR(B)$, why must it be so justified when I have? Why, if I do have such a $CR(B)$, must my decision to make B false be justified, if at all, by justifying that $CR(B)$, and not by whatever will in any case justify a dispositional $CR_B(A) = p$, or my belief that my $CR_B(A) = p$? To that question I know of no good answer.

IV

Conditional Bets

The impact on Bayesianism of the problems discussed in section III must not be exaggerated. Conditionalisation is a theory of how our credences should be updated in response to evidence. Whether this updating involves *deciding* what output credences to have is a moot point. If it does, conditionalisation is itself a decision theory. But even if it is, the problems discussed above do not apply to it. For they arise only when our trying to decide whether to make a proposition B true or false stops us having a non-zero credence in B or in ¬B. When B is new evidence, certain or uncertain, about some other proposition A, it automatically gives us a non-zero input credence in B: that after all is what makes B part of our evidence. In assessing Bayesianism as a theory of evidence, we may therefore set aside the questions raised for it by the decision theory of chapter 5.V.

This however still leaves us with the task of finding a general rationale for conditionalisation, given the limitations, discussed in sections I and II, of the pro rata rule and of Bayes's proposition 3. One possible rationale is provided by the idea of a *conditional bet*, an extension of the generalised idea of betting used in sections II and III of chapter 5 to justify a probability measure of degrees of belief. That idea, as we noted in chapter 8.II, only justifies constraints on credences that one person has at one time, e.g. that my simultaneous credences in A and in ¬A must always add up to 1. When evidence B changes my credence in A from a prior $CR(A)$ to a posterior $CR_B(A)$, our betting measure of belief imposes no such constraints on them: there is no betting reason why $CR(A)$, my prior credence in A, and $CR_B(¬A)$, my posterior credence in ¬A, should add up to 1. Nor should there be: constraints imposed on simultaneous credences by a betting measure of belief cannot be expected to limit the credences we can have at different times.

Some bets, however, do relate prior and posterior credences. These are the conditional bets where, for example, you bet me q units to win 1 if A is true, but only if B is also true; if B is false, the bet is off. If your attitude to this bet makes q measure a credence at all, it will be the credence $CR_B(A)$ that (you believe) you will have in A if you learn B. This being so, there may be some combination of bets, including conditional bets, on which one of us will lose whatever happens unless our prior and posterior credences on A, as measured by these betting odds, are related by conditionalisation. If there is, that may show conditionalisation to be the only rational rule for updating any $CR(A)$.

One such combination of bets has been said to show just this. Suppose your prior credence in A conditional on B, $CR(A | B)$, is q, the posterior credence you will actually have in A after learning that B is true, $CR_B(A)$, is q', and your prior credence in B, $CR(B)$, is p. These values are reflected in the following bets, made before you learn B:

(i)   a conditional bet: you pay q units to win 1 if A is true, iff B is true;
(ii) if B is true you will pay $1-q'$ units to win 1 if ¬A is true;
(iii) you pay $p(q-q')$ units to win $q-q'$ if B is true.

The odds in (i) and (ii) seem acceptable, given that q is your prior credence in A conditional on B and q' is the unconditional credence in A that you will have when you do learn B. The odds in (iii) should also be acceptable, as $q-q'$ simply fixes the size of the bet, leaving p to reflect your prior credence in B.

Now let us see how much you will gain or lose overall on these bets in each of the four possible situations: namely, that B and A are both true, B is true and A is false, A is true and B is false, and A and B are both false. Table 6 shows your gains on each bet, and your net gain, in each of these situations.

Your gains	if B and A	if B and ¬A	if ¬B and A	if ¬B and ¬A
on bet (i)	$1-q$	$-q$	0	0
on bet (ii)	$-(1-q')$	q'	0	0
on bet (iii)	$(1-p)(q-q')$	$(1-p)(q-q')$	$-p(q-q')$	$-p(q-q')$
net	$p(q'-q)$	$p(q'-q)$	$p(q'-q)$	$p(q'-q)$

Table 6

This tells us that if $q' > q$, i.e. if learning B makes your posterior credence $CR_B(A)$ exceed $CR(A|B)$, your prior credence in A conditional on B, you will win overall whatever happens; while if $q' < q$, i.e. if learning B makes your $CR_B(A)$ less than $CR(A|B)$, you will lose whatever happens. So in either case one party to this combination of bets will lose whatever happens, a situation which we agreed in chapter 5.III removes the whole point of betting. Only if $q' = q$, so that

(7.4) $CR_B(A) = CR(A|B)$,

as conditionalisation requires, will that situation not arise.

Does this argument work? Arguably not, since it assumes that q, your betting quotient or cost/benefit (c/b) ratio for the conditional bet (i), measures your $CR(A|B)$, your conditional credence in A given B. Here, that assumption seems to beg the question. For what your c/b ratio for bet (i) really seems to measure is what you now *think* your credence in A would be if you learned B, i.e. what you now believe your $CR_B(A)$ to be. If so, then all the argument shows is that, unless this belief of yours is true, i.e. unless your $CR_B(A)$ *will* be what you now *think* it will be, so that $q = q'$, one of us will lose money whatever happens. It does not show that one of us will lose money unless your *actual* $CR_B(A)$ – or what you now believe it to be – is equal to $CR(A|B)$, which is what needs to be shown to justify conditionalisation.

V

Imaging

We have seen why the arguments considered in this chapter fail to show that conditionalisation is always right. Their failure does not, however, show that it is often or even ever wrong. For even if it does not follow from some independent principle of rationality, the plausibility of its prescriptions may still recommend it as a general rule. If we do need a rule for updating our credences in response to evidence, what other rule is there?

To that rhetorical question there is at least one possible answer, at least for basic conditionalisation, where the input credence in our evidence B is 1. The answer is *imaging*, which is an alternative to the pro rata rule and best described in the sample space terminology of section I. Put in those terms, the pro rata rule derives probabilities posterior to B by redistributing the prior probabilities of all the sample points that B rules out pro rata over all the points that it does not rule out. Imaging by contrast adds the *whole* prior probability of each ruled-out point to the one remaining point that represents the possible world which is most like that of the ruled-out point.

To see how this works, suppose a coin toss may land heads (H), tails (T) or on edge (E), and let these be the points of a sample space {H,T,E}, with our prior credences in them being 0.5, 0.4 and 0.1 respectively. Now suppose we learn that the coin toss did *not* land heads. How should we distribute our prior credence 0.5 in the ruled-out point H over the two remaining points T and E?

The pro rata rule tells us that, since our prior credence in T is four times that in E, our posterior credences should be

$$\text{CR}_{\neg H}\{T\} = 0.4 + 0.5 \times (4/5) = 0.8 \text{ and}$$
$$\text{CR}_{\neg H}\{E\} = 0.1 + 0.5 \times (1/5) = 0.2.$$

To see how imaging differs from this, suppose we think that a world where our coin toss lands heads is more like one where it lands tails than one where it lands on edge. If this is true, imaging tells us to add not four-fifths but *all* our prior credence in H to our prior credence in T, thus making our posterior credences

$$\text{CR}_{\neg H}\{T\} = 0.4 + 0.5 \times 1 = 0.9 \text{ and}$$
$$\text{CR}_{\neg H}\{E\} = 0.1 + 0.5 \times 0 = 0.1.$$

Which of these two rules gives the right answer? In this case perhaps imaging does; but certainly not always. Take the example of section I where my short-sighted observation of a throw of a die rules out the results 1, 2 and 3 and raises my previously equal credences in 4, 5 and 6 unequally. If conditionalising is wrong here, as the example suggests, imaging is worse. For the reason my blurred vision raises my prior credence in 4 less than my credences in 5 and 6 is that it shows me how *black* the top face of the die is. But in this respect face 4, with fewer black spots than 5 or 6, resembles the ruled-out faces 1, 2 and 3 more than either 5 or 6 does. So imaging here would *only* raise my prior credence in 4, leaving my prior credences in 5 and 6 unchanged: a prescription that is even less credible than conditionalising.

Imaging, in short, like conditionalisation, seems to give the right answer in some cases and not in others. This does not, however, put the two rules on a par, because it is rarely clear how to apply the imaging rule. We saw in chapter 6.V that the evidential application of Bayes's Theorem is largely limited to credences by the generally insoluble problem of finding knowable objective priors. But applying imaging faces the usually even less answerable question of which possible world is closest to that of each sample point excluded by our evidence. Only in a few artificial cases, such as the die-throwing and coin-tossing examples just given, is this at all obvious. Generally, there being no clear answer to this question, the imaging rule yields no prescription at all.

Bayesianism faces no such problems, and even when its prescriptions seem implausible, at least it is clear what they are. In the absence of any equally widely applicable and more plausible rival, it may therefore reasonably claim to be the best if not the only evidential game in town. As such, it may even claim to override the intuitions appealed to in presenting apparent counter-examples. Perhaps these are as erroneous as the so-called 'gambler's fallacy' (which makes a long run of heads *lower* our credence in heads on the next toss), or the pre-theoretical idea that whales are fish. For just as our best theory of biology is entitled to reject that idea, so Bayesianism, as our best theory of evidence, may be entitled to reject a few unrationalised conflicting intuitions.

VI

Non-Bayesian Behaviour

The analogy just drawn between Bayesianism and other scientific theories is not, however, as close as it may at first appear. There are after all independent reasons for reclassifying whales with land-based animals that breathe and breed in the way that whales do and (other) fish do not. We have not so far seen any equally independent reasons to require credences to be updated by conditionalisation. In particular, if no independently compelling principles of rationality entail the Bayesian rule, the non-Bayesian responses to evidence that we have seen to be plausible in some cases can hardly be rejected as irrational.

Similarly for more serious examples of non-Bayesian behaviour reported by various authors. In one well-known example, given by Tversky and Kahneman (1982), people were presented with the following story and question:

> A cab was involved in a hit and run accident at night. Two cab companies, the Green and the Blue, operate in the city. You are given the following data:
>
> (a) 85% of the cabs in the city are Green and 15% are Blue;

(b) a witness identified the cab as Blue. ... [U]nder the same circumstances ... the witness correctly identified each one of the two colours 80% of the time and failed 20% of the time.

What is the probability that the cab involved in the accident was Blue rather than Green? (p. 156)

The authors report that

A large number of subjects have been presented with slightly different versions of this problem, with very consistent results. The ... answer is typically 0.80, a value which coincides with the credibility of the witness and is apparently unaffected by the relative frequency of Blue and Green cabs. (p. 157)

Since this answer seems to rely only on the reliability of the witness (whom I shall call Jim), it seems to be *reliabilist* in the sense of chapter 8.III. But whatever it is, it differs markedly from the Bayesian answer. The latter allows for datum (a) above by assuming prior credences $CR(B) = 0.15$ in the hypothesis B that the cab was Blue, and $CR(G) = 0.85$ in the hypothesis G that it was Green. It allows for (b) by assuming prior conditional credences $CR(W \mid B) = 0.80$ and $CR(W \mid G) = 0.20$, where W says that Jim identifies the cab as Blue. Then, since the complex form of Bayes's Theorem given in chapter 7.VI tells us here that

$$P(B \mid W) = \frac{P(W \mid B) \times P(B)}{P(W \mid B) \times P(B) + P(W \mid G) \times P(G)},$$

these assumptions make the Bayesian rule prescribe the posterior credence

$$(9.8) \quad CR_W(B) = \frac{0.80 \times 0.15}{0.80 \times 0.15 + 0.20 \times 0.85} = 0.41,$$

and hence the conclusion that, as Tversky and Kahneman put it,

In spite of the witness's report ... the hit-and-run cab is more likely to be Green than Blue, because the base rate [of 85% Green cabs to 15% Blue] is more extreme than the witness is credible. (p. 157)

This case shows just how serious the difference between Bayesian and other responses to evidence can be: the criminal conviction of a cab driver on a charge of dangerous driving or worse could depend on it. The rationality or otherwise of Bayesianism matters not only in theory but in real life.

What then can be said for Bayesianism in this case? We saw in chapter 8.III that Bayesians could consistently deny the evidential value of an input credence $CR(B) = 1$ unless B has a minimum chance, say 0.95 or 0.99, of being true. Thus before admitting Jim's belief in B as evidence, even Bayesians could require the perceptual process which produced it to be reasonably reliable, in the sense of giving it no more than, say, a 0.05 or 0.01 chance of being false.

Now in the cab case we are told that, in the circumstances, Jim is right 80% of the time about whether the cabs he sees are Blue or Green. Suppose we equate this frequency with a chance, as we are clearly expected to do. Then we may infer that Jim's observation has an 80% chance of giving him a true belief about a cab's colour and thus a 20% chance of giving him a false one. This chance of error may be too high for Jim's testimony to meet standard 95% or 99% criteria of reliability, but it is not too high here because, since we know what it is, we can use it to derive our own credence in B. The only question is *how* we should use it.

Let us start by recalling the chances-as-evidence principle (CE) that, if our evidence about any proposition A is that $CH(A) = p$, our $CR(A)$ should also be p. So in this case, if our evidence is that Jim's full belief in B has an 80% chance of being true, our credence in B should be 0.80. Put like this, the reliabilist response of Tversky's and Kahneman's subjects seems both rational and right.

This however is not the end of the matter, since we noted in chapter 6.IV that (CE) as stated there holds only when no *other* proposition, that is available as evidence when neither A nor ¬A is, is evidence for a value of $CH(A)$ other than p. But in this case other evidence *is* available, which seems to entail a different value of $CH(B)$, namely a 15% chance that the cab which Jim saw was Blue. We must infer this chance from the given proportions of Blue and Green cabs if they are to be relevant; for what other bearing can the colours of other cabs have on Jim's prospects of being right about the colour of this one? But if we do infer this chance, we now have two values for $CH(B)$: 0.15, from the proportions of Blue and Green cabs; and 0.80, from Jim's track record of true observations. How can we derive a credence in B from these apparently conflicting data?

First, we must realise that these data are not really contradictory. A proposition can easily have more than one chance of being true, on any of the main views of chance discussed in chapters 3 and 4. This is most obvious on frequency views, where different chances are simply different frequencies in different reference classes: in this case a class of cabs on the one hand, and of Jim's observations of their colour on the other.

The question then is not how to reconcile our two values, 0.15 and 0.80, of $CH(B)$, but what credence in B, if any, we should derive from them. For while it may not matter that B can have two different chances of being true, it matters a great deal, as we have noted, that the same evidence can apparently justify two different credences in B. How then, if at all, can we apply a chances-as-evidence principle like (CE) in this case? Sometimes, when different pieces of evidence credit a proposition with different chances, the total evidence principle of chapter 6.II will tell us which to use. If new evidence about a seemingly fair coin toss reveals a previously hidden variable which gives it a different chance p of landing heads (H), then our $CR(H)$ given that evidence should be p. The new value p supersedes $CH(H)$'s other value, 0.5, because it is entailed by our *total* evidence about H, which $CH(H) = 1/2$ is not.

Unfortunately, the total evidence principle does not help us in our cab case, where neither of the chances with which different parts of our evidence credit B, 0.15 and 0.80, supersedes the other: there is no single value of $CH(B)$ that our total evidence entails. This makes it unclear which of these credences in B, if either, a reliabilist should recommend. It may also explain why, in practice, the response of Tversky and Kahneman's subjects depended on how the data was put to them. When for example they replaced their statement (a) above with (a′) Although the two companies are roughly equal in size, 85% of cab accidents in the city involve Green drivers and 15% involve Blue drivers,

they reported that

The answers to this problem were highly variable, but the base rate was no longer ignored. The median answer was 0.60, which lies between the reliability of the witness (0.80) and the correct answer (0.41). (p. 157)

VII

Conclusion

What should we make of the results reported in section VI? In particular, should we conclude that, as Tversky and Kahneman assume, the Bayesian answer to their question is in fact the right one, despite the failure of most of their subjects to give it?

One reason for buying the Bayesian prescription in this hypothetical hit-and-run case is that, as (9.8) shows, it takes account in a simple and systematic way of all the apparently relevant data: both the witness's 80% reliability and the fact that 15% of the cabs, or of the cabs involved in accidents, are Blue. Reliabilism by contrast offers no such simple and obvious way of reconciling, choosing between or combining these two sets of data.

On the other hand, the fact that conditionalisation is easily applied in this case does not prove that it gives the right answer to it, especially as most of those to whom the case was put preferred a very different answer. We have also noted other cases, in earlier sections, where conditionalisation seems clearly to give the wrong answer; and others again, notably in decision-making, where it is as hard to apply as reliabilism is in the hit-and-run case. In both respects Bayesianism and reliabilism seem on a par, each being applicable or credible in different cases but neither in all. This is not a satisfactory conclusion, given the differences we have seen in their prescriptions in some of the cases to which both of them apply.

Finally, however, failing an unforeseen third way of resolving this dispute, we should recall one means by which Bayesians could settle it in their favour. We noted in chapter 8.III that

there are subjective surrogates for chances, which ... if they work at all ... can surely cope with any chances that may be needed to give input credences an external justification.

If these surrogates do work, Bayesians will in particular be able to replicate any reliabilist recipe for updating our credences in response to evidence. And if they can do that, then Bayesianism will certainly be a better bet than reliabilism. But can they do it? To answer that question we must first see exactly what it is they need to do.

Further Reading

The conditional bet argument for conditionalisation discussed in section IV is due to Lewis (1997) and was first reported in Teller (1973). For the imaging discussed in section V, see Lewis (1976), reprinted with a postscript in Lewis (1986).

For a survey of the literature on how probabilities of conditionals are related to conditional probabilities, see Hájek (2001), and Edgington (2001).

Other examples of non-Bayesian behaviour are described in Kahneman and Tversky (1974), reprinted in Moser (1990). Kahneman et al. (1982) also contains several other articles on the psychology of decision-making and of probabilistic inference.

10
Chance, Frequency and Credence

I

The Straight Rule

In chapters 3 and 4 we examined various views of chances, like the chances of coin tosses landing heads, of male or female births, of catching infectious diseases, or of radioactive atoms decaying in various periods of time. In all these examples, and on any view of chance, there is an undeniably close link between chances and such actual frequencies as the fractions of actual coin tosses that land heads, of births that are male, of people who catch diseases and of atoms that decay in any finite time.

Because these actual frequencies are physical, and also probabilities – since they satisfy the rules of numerical probability – they seem as entitled as anything else to be called chances. Yet as no one can deny that such frequencies exist, they cannot be what those who deny the existence of chances have in mind. What they deny are rather the *hypothetical limiting frequencies* that are entailed by what were argued in chapter 4 to be the three best theories of chance: the *modal chance* and *propensity* theories, and the theory that chances just *are* hypothetical limiting frequencies. Hence the decision in 4.VII, to call actual finite frequencies *statistical probabilities* rather than chances, made in order to keep the existence of chances a serious question, which otherwise it would not be. In reading what follows it is important to bear in mind this restriction on what is meant here by 'chance'.

How then are chances, so understood, linked to actual finite frequencies, or statistical probabilities, if not by being identical to them? It is evident that there is a link, and a close one, but less evident precisely what it is. Take a coin toss's chance $\mathrm{CH}(\mathrm{H})$ of landing heads. On the hypothetical limiting frequency view, $\mathrm{CH}(\mathrm{H})$ is the limiting frequency of heads, $f_\infty(\mathrm{H})$, in a hypothetical infinite set or *population* of tosses, of which any finite set of actual tosses is said to be a *sample*. (This use of 'sample' has nothing to do with the terminology of 'sample points' and 'sample spaces' introduced in chapter 2.IV.)

This view of chance makes $f_n(\mathrm{H})$, the frequency of heads in a finite sample of n actual tosses, our most direct estimate of $\mathrm{CH}(\mathrm{H})$, since $f_\infty(\mathrm{H})$ is by definition the limit, if any, of $f_n(\mathrm{H})$ as $n \to \infty$. This link between $f_n(\mathrm{H})$ and $f_\infty(\mathrm{H})$ might then be taken to justify the so-called *straight rule* of inference, from $f_n(\mathrm{H}) = p$ to $\mathrm{CH}(\mathrm{H}) = p$, on the grounds that in the long run, as n increases without limit, $f_n(H)$ will tend to equal $\text{CH}(H)$, if $\text{CH}(H)$ exists. This justification is, however, very weak, and not only because, as the economist Maynard Keynes said in a different context, 'in the long run we are all dead'. Another weakness of it is that many other rules have the same asymptotic property as the straight rule, since many functions of $f_n(H)$ also tend to $f_\infty(H)$ as $n \to \infty$: $f_n(H) + 1/n$ does, for example, since $1/n \to 0$ as $n \to \infty$. So while we may still prefer the straight rule because it is the simplest, that is no reason to think it more reliable then other rules with the same limit.

A slightly better case for the straight rule exploits the fact that we use it to estimate statistical probabilities as well as what I am calling chances. That is, we use it to estimate actual frequencies in finite populations when only samples of them have been observed. That this is an important use of the rule to estimate probabilities is shown by the practice of insurance companies. We saw in chapter 8.III that my chance $\text{CH}(A)$ of catching an infectious disease D is what matters to me when I am trying to decide what premium it is worth paying to insure myself against A's truth. But that chance is not, or not directly, what matters to my insurers. To them what matters is the actual frequency, among people who take out this insurance policy, of those who will catch D, since that is what determines whether the policy will make or lose them money. This is the real reason why insurers use frequencies to calculate what in 8.III I called their 'basic premiums' (i.e. what their premiums would be if they did not have to cover overheads and provide profits)'. But as the insurers cannot yet observe the frequency they want, namely the frequency $f_N(D)$ of D in the whole population of N potential clients, they must estimate it from the observable frequency $f_n(D)$ in a sample of n people who have already been exposed to D for more than its incubation period. And for this purpose the straight rule is not only the undoubted default, it is one for which we can now make a better than asymptotic case, as follows.

To state the case more generally, I shall adapt the symbolism of 8.III by letting $f_N(G/F)$ be, if N is finite, the frequency of things that are G in an actual total population of N things that are F or, if N is infinite, the limiting frequency of G-things in a total population of F-things that may only be hypothetical. Moreover, since 'F' serves only to specify this total population, we may abbreviate '$f_N(G/F)$' to '$f_N(G)$' and take that to mean the frequency of G-things in the population so specified. Similarly, $f_n(G)$ is the frequency of G-things in a sample of n *actual* members of that population. Then whether or not the total population is actual, and whether or not N is finite, the straight rule tells us to use $f_n(G)$ as our estimate of $f_N(G)$.

This wider application of the straight rule does give us a reason to prefer its estimate of $f_N(G)$ to others which, like $f_n(G) + 1/n$, also $\to f_\infty(G)$ as $N \to \infty$. For when the total population is actual and N is finite, then in principle, if rarely in practice, n may equal N: our sample may be the whole population. And when it is, only the straight rule will give us the true value of $f_N(G)$. So if, since we rarely know N when we know n and $f_n(G)$, we want a rule which, as n increases, could be right for all n, including $n=N$, only the straight rule will do.

However, even if the straight rule is right, it is rarely much use even when N is finite, and never when N is infinite, as it is when $f_N(G)$ is, or is entailed by, the chance CH (G). For when n is far less than N, as it must be in this case, and mostly is when N is finite, we need more than the fact that $f_n(G)$ is the best estimate of $f_N(G)$. We need to know how *good* an estimate it is, i.e. how *probable* it is for any given n that $f_n(G)$ equals, or is at least close to, $f_N(G)$. In particular, we need to know this when N is infinite, as it will be when $f_N(G)$ equals the chance CH (Ga) that any F-thing a has of being G, which is the case that concerns us here. What tells us what we need to know in this case is not the straight rule but a link that requires the so-called *strong law of large numbers*.

II

The Large Numbers Link

Let us assume that, in the terminology of section I, any F-thing a has a probability $P(Ga) = p$ of being G which is between 0 and 1. Then, however this probability is read, the strong law of large numbers says that, for any real numbers δ and ε, however small, between 0 and 1, there is a number N of F-things such that for all $n \geq N$, the probability (read in the same way) of p and $f_n(G)$ differing by more than δ is ε or less. And only if this law holds can we be sure that, for any given δ, ε will decrease (though never to 0) as n increases, which is the link between $f_n(G)$ and p that we need and which I shall call the *Large Numbers Link*, or LNL for short.

What we think LNL tells us depends on how we read $P(Ga)$. And if we read it as a chance, CH (Ga), what LNL tells us will also depend on which of the main views of chance we accept. On the *modal chance* view, ε tells us how *possible* it is for $f_n(G)$ to differ from p by more than δ: a possibility which, while it can never be 0, a large enough n can make as small as we like. On the *propensity* view, $1-\varepsilon$ measures a *disposition* of any sample of n F-things to yield, if endlessly repeated, a limiting frequency $1-\varepsilon$ of values of $f_n(G)$ that differ from p by no more than δ: a limiting frequency which, while it will never reach 1, a sufficiently large n will bring as close to 1 as we like. While on the *hypothetical limiting frequency* view, $1-\varepsilon$ just *is* the limiting frequency with which $f_n(G)$, in an endless sequence of hypothetical n-membered samples of F-things, will differ from p by not more than δ. In short, each of these three views of chance makes the same sense of the chance $1-\varepsilon$ as it makes of the original chance CH (Ga).

So far so good, *if* LNL holds: a serious proviso, since LNL is not entailed just by the existence of $P(Ga)$, not even if every other member of our population has the same probability p of being G. The best way to see why that is not enough, and why chances do have what it takes to satisfy LNL, is to use the terminology of sample spaces to generate, in the die-throwing case of chapter 7.II, new spaces to contain all the possible outcomes of several throws. This will help us to see how the probabilities of any outcome $\underline{O}$ of a single throw can be related to the frequency $f_n(O)$ of $\underline{O}$ in a sequence of n throws.

In chapter 7.II, the space $\{1,2,3,4,5,6\}$ of results of a single throw was called $\underline{K}$, instead of the more usual Ω used in chapter 2.IV to introduce the idea of sample spaces. That was to emphasise the dependence of this space on the background evidence K which tells us that one throw of a die will have one and only one – but may have any one – of these six results. It is after all contingent that this is so, since a die need not necessarily land with one face up: it might not land at all, or it might land on edge, with two faces equally uppermost. It is equally contingent that several throws of a die will result in just one (which may be any one) of the logically possible combinations of the possible results of a single throw. So as this is also in our background evidence K, however the probabilities of the results of our throws are interpreted, I shall still call our one-throw sample space $\underline{K}$, and will call our two-throw space $\underline{K}^2$, our three-throw space $\underline{K}^3$, and so on.

On these assumptions, if $\underline{K}$'s sample points are the results 1, 2, 3, 4, 5 or 6 of a single throw, $\underline{K}^2$'s points are the thirty-six possible *ordered pairs* of these results: $\langle 1,1 \rangle$, $\langle 1,2 \rangle$, ... , $\langle 2,1 \rangle$, $\langle 2,2 \rangle$, ... $\langle 6,5 \rangle$, $\langle 6,6 \rangle$. (The pairs are ordered because we need to distinguish, for example, getting 5 on the first throw and 3 on the second from getting 3 on the first and 5 on the second.) Similarly, $\underline{K}^3$'s points are all the ordered triples, $\langle 1,1,1 \rangle$ ... $\langle 6,6,6 \rangle$, of $\underline{K}$'s members; and so on. For any finite n, the points of the sample space $\underline{K}^n$ are all the so-called 'ordered n-tuples' of sample points of $\underline{K}$.

Having defined these new spaces, we can now identify certain outcomes of them with possible frequencies of outcomes of $\underline{K}$. Take for example the frequency $f_2\{3\}$ in two throws, i.e. in $\underline{K}^2$, of the outcome $\{3\}$ of $\underline{K}$: if both our throws land 3, $f_2\{3\} = 1$; if none do, $f_2\{3\} = 0$; and if one does, $f_2\{3\} = 1/2$. Now suppose that in fact $f_2\{3\} = 1/2$. This will be $f_2\{3\}$'s value just in case the result of the two throws is any ordered pair which, like $\langle 3,1 \rangle$ and $\langle 5,3 \rangle$ contains one and only one 3. But as these pairs are all sample points of the space $\underline{K}^2$, the set of them is a subset – an *outcome* – of the sample space $\underline{K}^2$, whose probability is therefore the probability that $f_2\{3\} = 1/2$. This means that for our purposes we can identify $f_2\{3\} = 1/2$ with this outcome of $\underline{K}^2$; $f_2\{3\} = 1$ with another outcome of $\underline{K}^2$, the simple outcome $\{\langle 3,3 \rangle\}$; and $f_2\{3\} = 0$ with the outcome whose members are all the ordered pairs in $\underline{K}^2$ which, like $\langle 5,6 \rangle$, contain *no* 3s.

Similarly with complex outcomes of $\underline{K}$, like $\{1,3,5\}$, getting an odd number. Its frequency in three throws, $f_3\{1,3,5\}$, is 1 if all three throws yield an odd number, $2/3$ if two do, $1/3$ if one does and 0 if none do. So here too every possible value of $f_3\{1,3,5\}$ is an outcome, in this case of the sample space $\underline{K}^3$. Thus the value $f_3\{1,3,5\}$ $= 1/3$ is the outcome of $\underline{K}^3$ whose members are all the points in $\underline{K}^3$ which, like $\langle 2,3,2 \rangle$, contain just one odd number. Similarly for every other possible value of $f_3\{1,3,5\}$ and, more generally, for every possible value in any space $\underline{K}^n$ of the frequency of any outcome $\underline{O}$ of $\underline{K}$. For any finite number n, and for every number m from 0 to n, the value $f_n(\underline{O}) = m/n$ is an outcome of the sample space $\underline{K}^n$.

This being so, we can fix the probability of any value of any $f_n(\underline{O})$ by fixing the probability of the outcome in $\underline{K}^n$ which is that value. How may we do this? The obvious starting point is $P(\underline{O})$, $\underline{O}$'s probability in $\underline{K}$, which we might hope to entail the probability that $f_n(\underline{O}) = m/n$ for all n and m. Surely, for example, if we know the probability of getting an odd number on any one throw of a die, we can deduce the probabilities of getting 0, 1, ... n odd numbers on n throws? Unfortunately not: the probabilities of $\underline{K}$'s outcomes will not fix the probabilities of all the outcomes in $\underline{K}^n$ – and in particular will not entail LNL – unless our n throws are *independent* in a sense which we have not yet sufficiently discussed.

III

Independence

The idea of independence was introduced in chapter 1.VII with the example of two coin tosses, each of whose probabilities of landing heads is $1/2$. I said there that, if A says that the *second* toss lands heads (H) rather than tails (T), and B says that the *first* one lands heads, then the tosses are probabilistically independent if and only if

(1.1) $P(A \wedge B) = P(A) \times P(B) = 1/2 \times 1/2 = 1/4$, and also if and only if
(1.3) $P(A \mid B) = P(A) = 1/2$.

In equating (1.1) and (1.3) we tacitly took for granted equation

(1.2) $P(A \mid B) = \dfrac{P(A \wedge B)}{P(B)}$,

not as the definition of $P(A \mid B)$ which we agreed in chapter 7.I to make it, but as a substantive claim which makes (1.3) say that 'B tells us nothing about A's prospects of being true'. What then does it take, in this case or any other, to make that claim true of $P(A)$ and $P(B)$?

To answer this question, we must first see why it is not enough, in order to make $P(A)$ and $P(B)$ satisfy (1.1) and (1.3), for their values to be equal. We can see this most quickly by taking B to be A's negation, $\neg A$. For then, if $P(A)$ is $1/2$, we have

$P(B) = P(\neg A) = 1 - P(A) = 1/2 = P(A)$ but
$P(A \wedge B) = P(A \wedge \neg A) = 0$ and
$P(A \mid B) = P(A \mid \neg A) = 0$,

thus falsifying both (1.1) and (1.3). While if B is A, when again

$P(B) = P(A)$,
$P(A \wedge B) = P(A \wedge A) = P(A)$ and
$P(A \mid B) = P(A \mid A) = 1$,

which falsifies both (1.1) and (1.3) for all $P(A)$ less than 1.

These two cases show why the mere fact that $P(A) = P(B)$ does not make either $P(A \wedge B)$ nor $P(A \mid B)$ a function of $P(A)$, since $P(A) = P(B)$ is consistent with values of $P(A \wedge B)$ and $P(A \mid B)$ ranging, as the cases illustrate, from 0 to 1. Moreover, since in our coin-tossing case A and B are made true by the same outcome ($\underline{H}$) of two different tosses, this result also shows why, in the sample space symbolism of section II, $\underline{H}$'s probability $P(H)$ in $\underline{K}$, the sample space of results of a single toss, will not fix the probability in $\underline{K}^2$ of $f_2(H) = 1$, i.e. the probability $P(A \wedge B)$ of getting heads on both tosses.

This is why our coin tosses need something other than equal chances of landing heads to make them independent. What in fact makes them independent is, as we noted in 1.VII, the fact that 'the result of the first toss does not physically affect the chance of heads on the second toss: the tosses are *physically* independent'. That is what makes the chances $CH(A)$ and $CH(B)$ satisfy (1.1) and (1.3). It is what makes $CH(A \mid B)$, A's conditional chance of being true given that B is, the same as A's unconditional chance $CH(A)$; and it is what makes $CH(A \wedge B)$, the chance that $f_2(H) = 1$, equal to $CH(A) \times CH(B)$.

The same physical independence of our coin tosses will also fix the chances of all other possible values of the frequency of heads, $f_n(H)$, for any n. In particular, it will make the chances of $f_n(H)$ being close to $CH(H)$ increase with n, as LNL says and as Figure 5 illustrates.

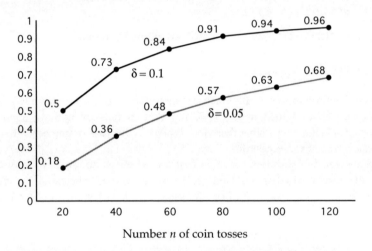

Number n of coin tosses

Figure 5: Chances of $f_n(H)$ lying within δ of $CH(H) = 1/2$

To enable us to make the point more generally, in sample space terms, let us call each toss of our coin an *instance* of our sample space $\underline{K}$ (which in this case we may take to be {H,T}); and similarly in other cases. Then what we assume is that the chance $CH(O)$ of any instance of any outcome $\underline{O}$ in any space $\underline{K}$ is physically independent of any *other* instance of any outcome in $\underline{K}$. If it is, then for all n, and all m from 0 to n, the chance in $\underline{K}^n$ that $f_n(O) = m/n$ will be fixed by $CH(O)$ in conformity with LNL.

IV

Chances and Estimates

In section III we assumed that, in our set of two or more coin tosses, the chances of heads on any pair of tosses are not only equal but independent in the sense of satisfying equations (1.1) and (1.3). This assumption is not a necessary truth: the result of one toss could affect the chance of heads on the next toss, for example by causing the coin to be bent one way if it lands heads and another if it lands tails. So if the assumption is true, it will, as we have noted, be made true by the contingent fact that the chance of any one toss landing heads is not affected by how any other toss lands.

To say that the chance CH(H) of heads on one member of a set of coin tosses is unaffected by the result of any other member is not to say that our *estimate* of CH(H) will not or should not be so affected. It might or it might not. We might for example have so much evidence of symmetry in the coin and in how it is tossed that our belief that CH(H) = 1/2 can and should survive almost any frequency of heads in almost any number of tosses: even, say, an unbroken run of fifty heads.

Usually, however, our estimates of chances will and should be affected by frequency evidence. The higher f_n(H) is for large n, the greater our estimate of CH(H) is apt to be. In particular, if all we know in advance is that all tosses have the *same* chance of landing heads, and are physically independent, we might use the straight rule of section I to derive a credence in CH(H) lying in an interval, centred on f_n(H), whose width will depend on how reliable our estimate needs to be. If for example we see 58 out of 120 tosses landing heads, so that f_{100}(H) = 0.48, data like those shown in Figure 5 above might make us let this frequency give us a credence of about 0.96 in CH(H) lying between 0.38 and 0.58: a credence that on the reliabilist theory of chapter 8.III can be justified by the 0.96 chance of f_{100}(H) lying within 0.1 of any CH(H) that is close to 1/2.

We should note here that it is not at all unusual to know that two chances are equal and independent without knowing what they are. Nor is this mixture of knowledge and ignorance peculiar to chance: it arises with all quantities related by theories containing empirical constants, like the theory which says that a gas's volume V is a function of its mass M, temperature T and pressure P, such as

$$V = kMT/P,$$

where k is a constant whose value varies from gas to gas. Given this theory, we can know that two physically independent samples of the same gas, whose equal masses, temperatures and pressures we know, will have the same volume V, even if we do not know what V is because we do not know what k is.

Similarly with chances, like the chance p_t of any atom of a given radioelement decaying, D, in any period of t years. We noted in chapter 4.IV that the theory of radioactivity gives this chance as

(4.3) $p_t = 1 - e^{-\lambda t}$,

where λ is a constant which has different values for different radioelements. As the theory itself does not tell us what these values are, we can know that two atoms of the same radioelement have equal values of p_t for all t even if we do not know what those values are, because we do not know what λ is. And the only way to find out λ for any given radioelement, such as radium, is to estimate p_t for various t by observing the frequency $f_t(D)$ with which atoms of the element decay within t.

Yet however much our best estimate of the chance CH(O) of any outcome O varies with O's frequency f_n(O) in n instances of CH(O), in order to justify its variation with f_n(O) we have had to assume that CH(O) itself does *not* vary with the results that fix f_n(O)'s values. In other words, we have assumed that, as well as the varying credences in O which various frequencies should give us, there is an unvarying objective chance CH(O) of which those frequencies are estimates. But to many Bayesians this looks like metaphysical overkill, to be dispensed with if possible, i.e. if we can get the same results, especially LNL, the Large Numbers Link, without making this assumption. And we can, as we shall now see.

V

Exchangeability

How can credences satisfy LNL if they are not, and should not be, independent of frequency evidence? The answer exploits the fact that independence, while sufficient to make probabilities satisfy LNL, is not necessary: a weaker condition called *exchangeability*, which credences can satisfy, will do the job. To see what this condition is, and how it works, let us look again at our coin-tossing example.

Consider the following sequence S_{10} of the outcomes of ten coin tosses:

Toss no:	1	2	3	4	5	6	7	8	9	10
Result:	H	H	T	T	T	H	T	T	H	T

where H is heads and T is tails. As before, we take all ten tosses to share whatever property or properties affect the credence CR(H) that I should have in any one toss landing heads. Only now, if we are not to beg the present question, that property cannot be the chance CH(H). Here we must take it that our tosses have and share only *non*-chance properties, and that these include everything relevant to what my CR(H) should be. This being so, then since every toss is the same as every other in all relevant respects, it cannot matter in what order we list their outcomes. So suppose for example we generate a new sequence S_{10}' by simply reordering the heads and tails in S_{10} as follows:

S_{10}' order:	1	2	3	4	5	6	7	8	9	10
S_{10} order:	5	2	7	1	9	8	3	6	10	4
Result:	T	H	T	H	H	T	T	H	T	T

Then my credence in S_{10}' should equal my credence in S_{10}, whatever it may be, as should my credence in any other ten-membered sequence of heads and tails that differs from S_{10} only in the order of its members. In other words, *exchanging* any members of any sequence $S_{10}*$ with the same frequency $f_{10}(H) = 0.4$ of heads as S_{10} should never change my credence in it: hence the term 'exchangeability'.

Next, we observe that the outcome $f_{10}(H) = 0.4$ in the sample space $\underline{K}^{10}$ is the set of all $S_{10}*$ sequences, each of which is a sample point of $\underline{K}^{10}$. So my credence in $f_{10}(H) = 0.4$ should be my credence in S_{10} multiplied by the number of $S_{10}*$ sequences, i.e. by the number of ways of getting four heads on ten tosses. And similarly for every other n, and every possible value of $f_n(H)$.

This constraint which a belief in exchangeability puts on our credences in the possible values of $f_n(H)$ for any n is weaker than that imposed by independence. But it is still strong enough to make these credences satisfy LNL, which is all that matters here. For, to revert to the discussion of section I, suppose we take an n-membered sample of our population of F-things, of which some are G and some are not, and number its members in some arbitrary way to generate an analogue of S_n, with 'H' and 'T' replaced by 'G' and '¬G'. By ordering our sample in this way, we have added information which we take to be irrelevant, since we think that all that matters is how many G-things the sample contains, not which things they are. In other words, we take the members of our analogue of S_n to be *exchangeable*, whether or not we think they have any objective chance of being G. And as that makes our credences in F-things being G satisfy LNL, we may now be able to say, without invoking chances, what, given $f_n(G)$, our credence that any F-thing is G should be. Let us see if we can.

VI

Frequencies and Credences

There is a link between credences and frequencies that does not rely on chances or even on exchangeability. Imagine a finite sequence of n coin tosses, and let A_i say that the ith toss lands heads, where $1 \le i \le n$. Now suppose I have the same credence $\text{CR}(A_i)$ in all A_i: $\text{CR}(H)$, the chance that each toss has of landing heads. How many of these tosses should I expect to land heads? One answer, given by the *finite frequency theorem*, is that the expected number of heads in n tosses is $n \times \text{CR}(H)$, thus making $\text{CR}(H)$ the expected value of the frequency $f_n(H)$ for all n.

This, however, only shows that $\text{CR}(H)$ is the *expected* value of $f_n(H)$ in the sense of 'expected' used in the decision theory of chapter 5.V. It need not be the actual or even a possible value of $f_n(H)$. For while $\text{CR}(H)$'s value can be any real number between 0 and 1, $f_n(H)$'s value can, as we have often noted, only be m/n for some whole number m between 0 and n. Thus suppose for example you think that each of three coin tosses is fair, so that your credence $\text{CR}(H)$, and hence your expected value of $f_3(H)$, is $1/2$. This cannot possibly be the actual frequency $f_3(H)$ of heads in three tosses, since that can only be $0, 1/3, 2/3$ or 1.

We therefore cannot read 'my expected value of $f_n(H)$ is CR(H)' as 'I should expect $f_n(H)$ to equal CR(H)', meaning that my credence in $f_n(H) = $ CR(H) should be 1. That is not true, and is not what the finite frequency theorem says. In fact the theorem can no more tell us what my credence in $f_n(H) = m/n$ should be for any given CR(H) than can the straight rule of section I. What we need to tell us that is LNL, as in the following example which, to avoid begging the question, I shall again state without saying how the probabilities in it are to be read.

In chapter 7.VI we saw how to use the complex form of Bayes's Theorem,

$$(7.15)\ \text{P}(A_i|B) = \frac{\text{P}(B|A_i) \times \text{P}(A_i)}{\sum_i \text{P}(B|A_i) \times \text{P}(A_i)},$$

to get the posterior probability $\text{P}(A_1|B_2) = 0.8$ of the hypothesis A_1 that a coin is double-headed, given that if A_1 is false, the coin is unbiased (A_2), A_1's prior probability $\text{P}(A_1)$ is 0.5, and B_2 says that both of $n = 2$ tosses land heads. Similarly for other values of $\text{P}(A_1)$ and of the number n of tosses that all land heads, as Figure 6 shows for $\text{P}(A_1) = 0.1$ as well as $\text{P}(A_1) = 0.5$, and for values of n from 0 to 6, where $\text{P}(A_1|B_0)$ is A_1's prior probability $\text{P}(A_1)$.

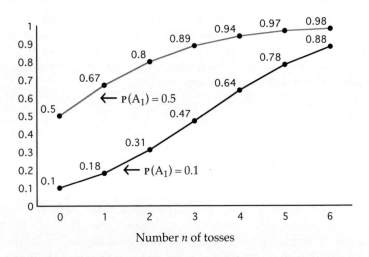

Figure 6: Posterior probability of A_1 if n tosses all land heads

From Figure 6 we can now derive the posterior probability of H, the hypothesis that any one of our coin tosses lands heads, given the evidence B_n of n heads in a row. We can do this by adapting equation

$$(7.14)\ \ \text{P}(B) = \sum_i \text{P}(B|A_i) \times \text{P}(A_i)$$

from chapter 7.VI, with $B = H$, two hypotheses, A_1 and A_2, and background B_n, so that

$$\text{P}(H|B_n) = \text{P}(H|A_1 \wedge B_n) \times \text{P}(A_1|B_n) + \text{P}(H|A_2 \wedge B_n) \times (1 - \text{P}(A_1|B_n)),$$

with H's prior probability $\text{P}(H) = \text{P}(H|B_0)$ being given by

$$P(H) = P(H \mid A_1) \times P(A_1) + P(H \mid A_2) \times (1 - P(A_1))$$

which, for $P(A_1) = 0.1$ and 0.5 respectively, gives $P(H)$ the values 0.55 and 0.75 shown below in Figure 7.

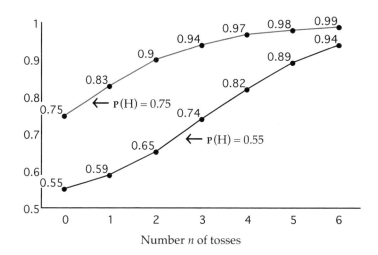

Figure 7: Posterior probability of H if n tosses all land heads

If this is our example, the question that faces us is how to make sense of it without reading any of its probabilities as chances. How, in particular, can we do this if A_1 and A_2 postulate values of the *chance* CH(H) of each toss landing heads? The answer is that we need not read A_1 and A_2 in that way. We can read them as being not about chances but, as in section V, about relevant *non*-chance properties of the coin and of the toss. That is, we can take A_2 to say that all these properties are symmetrical, thus justifying equal credences in heads and tails and thereby justifying CR(H) = 0.5. While in order to justify CR(H) = 1, A_1 need only say that the coin is double-headed: it need not add that there is a chance CH(H) = 1.

Nor, as we have seen, do we need chances to make us take the results of our sequence of n tosses of the coin to be exchangeable in the sense of section V, and thereby to make our credences satisfy LNL. And with LNL, A_1 and A_2 can justify credences in all possible values of $f_n(H)$, including $f_n(H) = 1$, for all n: A_1 trivially justifying CR($f_n(H)=1$) = 1 and A_2 justifying CR($f_n(H)=1$) = 0.5^n. Therefore, if our evidence B_n is that n tosses all land heads, i.e. that $f_n(H) = 1$, then we know that

$$\text{CR}(B_n \mid A_1) = 1 \text{ and } \text{CR}(B_n \mid A_2) = 0.5^n,$$

which is enough to enable a purely subjective reading of Figures 6 and 7 above.

VII

Subjectivism

The example worked out in section VI is both trivial and unrealistic. But it serves its purpose, which is to show as simply as possible how a subjective surrogate for chance works. For it shows not only how to derive posterior credences from prior ones by conditionalisation, but how to do so via simulated inferences from and to chances: e.g. from a fairly tossed coin's chance of landing heads to the chances of its doing so with any given frequency in any finite number of tosses.

Let us grant then that a subjective surrogate for chance exists. This in itself does not show that subjectivism is right, and that there are no objective chances. That needs more argument, especially about how well prior credences can fill the role of the chances they simulate. The problem, as always, is that input credences need justifying, and chances do not: they just need to exist. Thus on the objective reading of our coin tosses, each of them has a chance $CH(H)$ of landing heads that is either $1/2$, if the toss is unbiased, or 1, if it is of a double-headed coin. Whichever it is, there is no question of justifying this chance: it just *is*. Only *estimates* of it derived from frequencies need justifying, a justification which, on the reliabilist view sketched in chapter 8.III, the chance itself can provide, via the chances of frequencies that it entails.

On a subjective reading of the example, by contrast, any prior credence $CR(H)$ in heads on a single toss does need justifying. Otherwise the posterior credence $CR(H \mid B_n)$ may not be justified, since this can vary as much with $CR(H)$ as with $f_n(H)$. Thus, as Figure 7 above shows, $f_2(H) = 1$, two heads in a row, will make $CR(H \mid B_2) = 0.9$ if $CR(H) = 0.75$ but only 0.65 if $CR(H) = 0.55$. So which of these two values of $CR(H \mid B_2)$ is justified depends on which of these two priors is justified. What then, for a subjectivist, determines which of them – if either – *is* justified?

The standard subjectivist reply to this question is that our prior credences need *no* justification, beyond the fact that we have them. The idea that they do only arises because we share so many posterior credences derived from priors by conditionalisation on frequencies in large samples. This is especially true of the credences we get, via the chances-as-evidence principle (CE) of chapter 6.IV, from the chances which figure in laws of nature, like those of radioactive decay. But for subjectivists, our belief in the chances that laws seem to contain is not a cause but an effect of our having similar credences in their consequents, a similarity which subjectivists offer to explain as follows.

If, in Figure 7, the variation of the posterior probability $P(H \mid B_n)$ with the prior $P(H)$ is strikingly large when n is small, $P(H \mid B_n)$'s convergence on $f_n(H) = 1$ as n becomes large is more striking still. It only takes six heads in a row to turn $P(H)$s of 0.75 and 0.55 respectively into $P(H \mid B_6)$s, of 0.99 and 0.94, which are far closer to $f_6(H) = 1$ and to each other than are the priors they come from. And similarly, in other cases, for other frequencies and for other prior probabilities, large and small, provided only that the latter are neither 0 nor 1. For if LNL holds, a large enough n will bring the posteriors of all such prior probabilities as close as we like to $f_n(H)$ and thereby to each other. And all we need do to make LNL hold when these probabilities are credences is to think that the results which give $f_n(H)$ its value are exchangeable: chances are not called for. This, subjectivists say, is why many of our posterior credences are so close to the frequencies we have observed that we mistake them for chances: the shared frequency evidence to which they are posterior has swamped any differences in our prior credences.

How good is this as a defence of the claim that our prior credences need no justifying? LNL does indeed entail that however little we want our posterior credence in H to differ from $f_n(H)$, say by less than a small amount δ, *any* given non-zero prior credence in H will, if n is large enough, be turned by $f_n(H)$ into a posterior credence that is within δ of $f_n(H)$.

On the other hand, it is also true that, for any given n, *some* priors will *not* yield posteriors within δ of $f_n(H)$. Thus suppose that in our coin-tossing case we want our posterior $CR(H|B_n)$ to reach 0.9 if $f_n(H) = 1$. Then for any n, however large, there is some value of our prior $CR(A_1)$ in A_1, the hypothesis that our coin is double-headed, below which our posterior $CR(H|B_n)$ will be *less* than 0.9. This minimal prior may be small, and diminish rapidly with n, as Figure 8 shows, but for no value of n will it ever reach zero; and nor will it for any other non-zero $CR(H|B_n)$.

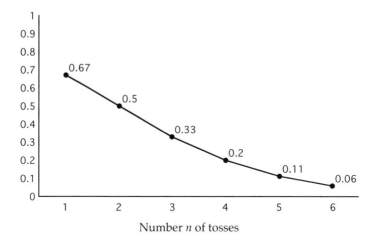

Figure 8: Greatest $CR(A_1)$ for which $CR(H|B_n) \leq 0.9$

It seems then that no non-zero posterior credence in H can be justified by any frequency evidence unless *some* non-zero prior credence in H is justified in some other way. This, plus the fact that conditionalising on evidence never raises to 1 our posterior credences in propositions it does not entail (nor raises zero prior credences in them at all), presents subjectivists with hard questions, to which they may respond in various ways. One is to repeat that, appearances to the contrary, prior credences need no justifying, perhaps on the internalist grounds of chapter

8.II that only credences can justify credences, that internal justification must start somewhere and that prior credences are where it starts. Another is to admit that prior credences can have external justification provided that, as in Nozick's theory of 8.III, it involves no chances. To these or other responses they may also add that other theories of evidence face problems too, which may be even worse. But whatever the rights and wrongs of that general debate, I shall say no more about it, since it is unlikely to turn on issues peculiar to probability.

In any case, however that debate may go, the subjectivist explanation of why we often have similar credences in the same propositions provokes two further questions. One is whether the explanation is true. Do we in fact get our shared credences by conditionalising on shared frequency or other evidence? If we do not, then the fact that if we did, this would explain our shared credences is like the fact that if the earth was flat, this would explain the landscape of East Anglia. Since the flat earth hypothesis is in fact false, it explains nothing, neither the flatness of Norfolk nor anything else. Similarly with the subjectivist explanation of how we get our credences: it will only explain those credences if it is true. Yet the evidence for it is, as we saw in chapter 9.VI, very uncertain: too many of us seem too often to behave in non-Bayesian ways. This may be irrational, as Bayesians claim, but that is irrelevant, since the question here is how we get the credences we actually have, not the credences we ought to have.

Still, our failure to conditionalise may not matter, provided most of us update many of our credences in ways, whatever they are, whose effects are close to those of conditionalisation. If we do, as the popularity of Bayesian models of confirmation suggests we may, our response to frequency evidence may still conform, if only approximately, to LNL. And this will then suffice to explain the similarity of our credences in the propositions which we therefore take to have corresponding chances of being true.

The other question which the subjectivist explanation of our posterior credences raises is how far, even if it is true, it supports subjectivism. The fact, if it is a fact, that we update our credences by conditionalising on non-chance evidence does not show that there are no chances. For as we saw in chapters 3 and 4, the main reason for postulating chances is not that they explain posterior *credences*, which is what conditionalisation aims to do, but that they explain *frequencies*. The frequencies of male and female births, of cancer among smokers and non-smokers, of radium atoms decaying in various intervals of time: if these can be explained at all, they can only be explained by chances. Conditionalisation on observed frequencies in samples of size n may indeed give us credences in propositions about frequencies in a larger but finite population of size N: as in Figure 6 above, which shows how my seeing only six coin tosses all land heads can give me a credence 0.98 in A_1, which says that $f_N(H) = 1$ for all N. Similarly then in other cases, and for other values of $f_N(H)$: if n is large enough, my seeing that $f_n(H) = m/n$ may give me a credence in a true proposition B_N about $f_N(H)$ – say that $f_N(H)$ lies between 0.5 and 0.7 – which is close enough to 1 to count as a full belief in B_N.

But my having a high posterior credence in B_N, i.e. my $\mathrm{CR}(B_N|f_n(H)=m/n)$ being close to 1, does not explain why B_N is *true*, any more than my input credence $\text{CR}(f_n(\text{H})=m/n) \approx 1$ explains why $f_n(\text{H}) = m/n$. On the contrary: my seeing that $f_n(\text{H}) = m/n$ is what explains my input credence $\text{CR}(f_n(\text{H})=m/n) \approx 1$ and thence, via conditionalisation, my posterior credence in B_N. If anything explains why $f_n(\text{H}) = m/n$ and why $0.5 < f_N(\text{H}) < 0.7$, it is the fact, if it is a fact, that H has a chance $\text{CH}(\text{H})$ which is near enough to 0.6.

This I believe to be the main objection to subjectivism: credences, however caused, cannot explain facts about actual frequencies. Only chances in the end can do that. If determinism is true, there will admittedly be piecemeal explanations of finite frequencies. Thus suppose that, in a sequence of six coin tosses, the first lands heads and all the others land tails. Suppose also that, besides the properties that all six tosses share, a 'hidden variable' G determines which way each one will land: heads if G's value is G_H and tails if its value is G_T. Then the fact that the first toss has the property G_H explains why it lands heads, and the fact that the others have the property G_T explains why they land tails. And the conjunction of these facts certainly entails, and perhaps explains, the fact that $f_6(\text{H}) = 1/6$. But if this is an explanation of that fact, it is not very enlightening, since what makes it work is the fact that $f_6(G_\text{H})$, the frequency of tosses with the property G_H, is also $1/6$. And what explains this fact, if not another frequency, this time of the deterministic causes that give a toss the property G_H, and so on and so on? Only a chance of H, or of G_H, or ... , can stop this otherwise endless regress of frequencies by explaining facts about $f_6(\text{H})$, or $f_6(G_\text{H})$, or ... without postulating yet more frequencies.

In short, just as many subjectivists think that only credences can justify credences, so they must all think that frequencies can only be explained by other frequencies. As neither view is either self-evident or entailed by a commitment to conditionalisation, it can only be motivated by some other objection to chances, such as positivism or Ockham's razor, the instruction not to multiply entities beyond necessity. But positivist objections to chances are no more credible than they are to other 'theoretical' entities, including the very credences that subject-ivists must accept; while I think that a better instruction than Ockham's is not to multiply entities beyond *reality*: a reality which in earlier chapters we have seen reason to believe contains both credences and chances.

Further Reading

For discussion of, and references to literature about, the straight rule of section I, see chapter 10 of Kyburg (1970). For a statement of the relevant law of large numbers, and a proof that exchangeability entails it, see de Finetti (1937), chapter 3. See also Skyrms (1980), part I, which argues for equating apparent chances with resilient credences, i.e. with credences that vary little under condition-alisation. For the finite frequency theorem, see Jeffrey (1985). Chapter 13 of Howson and Urbach (1993) offers a Bayesian reconstruction of von Mises's (1957) theory of chance, and chapter 15 defends Bayesian subjectivism generally against a wide range of other objections.

References

Where a reference contains two dates, the first date is that of first publication, the second that of the publication cited.

Adams, R. M. (1974) 'Theories of Actuality', in *The Possible and the Actual*, ed. M. J. Loux, Ithaca: Cornell University Press (1979), 190–209.

Armstrong, D. M. (1973) *Belief, Truth and Knowledge*, Cambridge: Cambridge University Press.

— (1983) *What is a Law of Nature?*, Cambridge: Cambridge University Press.

— (1993) *A Materialist Theory of the Mind*, rev. edn, New York: Routledge.

Ayer, A. J. (1956) 'What is a Law of Nature?', in his *The Concept of a Person and Other Essays*, London: Macmillan (1963), 209–34.

Baldwin, T. (1990) *G. E. Moore*, London: Routledge.

Bayes, T. (1763) 'An Essay Towards Solving a Problem in the Doctrine of Chances', in *Bayes's Theorem*, ed. R. G. Swinburne, Oxford: Oxford University Press (2002), 123–49.

Blackburn, S. (1973) *Reason and Prediction*, Cambridge: Cambridge University Press.

Carnap, R. (1945) 'The Two Concepts of Probability', *Philosophy and Phenomenological Research* 5, 513–32.

— (1955) 'Statistical and Inductive Probability', in *The Structure of Scientific Thought*, ed. E. H. Madden, Boston: Houghton Mifflin, 269–79.

— (1971) 'Inductive Logic and Rational Decisions', in *Studies in Inductive Logic and Probability*, vol. 1, ed. R. Carnap and R. C. Jeffrey, Berkeley: University of California Press, 5–31.

Carnap, R. and Jeffrey, R. C., eds (1971) *Studies in Inductive Logic and Probability*, vol. 1, Berkeley: University of California Press.

Christensen, D. (1991) 'Clever Bookies and Coherent Beliefs', *Philosophical Review* 100, 229–47.

Dancy, J. (1985) *Introduction to Contemporary Epistemology*, Oxford: Blackwell.

—, ed. (1988) *Perceptual Knowledge*, Oxford: Oxford University Press.

Davidson, D. (1970) 'Mental Events', in his *Essays on Actions and Events*, Oxford: Clarendon Press (1980), 207–25.

Earman, J. (1992) *Bayes or Bust? A Critical Examination of Bayesian Confirmation Theory*, Cambridge, Mass.: MIT Press.

Edgington, D. (2001) 'Conditionals', in *The Blackwell Guide to Philosophical Logic*, ed. L. Goble, Oxford: Blackwell, 385–415.

Eells, E. (1982) *Rational Decision and Causality*, Cambridge: Cambridge University Press.

Feigl, H. and Sellars, W., eds (1949) *Readings in Philosophical Analysis*, New York: Appleton-Century-Crofts.

Feller, W. (1957) *An Introduction to Probability Theory and Its Applications*, 2nd edn, New York: Wiley.

Finetti, B. de (1937) 'Foresight: its Logical laws, its Subjective Sources', in *Studies in Subjective Probability*, ed. H. E. Kyburg, Jr and H. E. Smokler, New York: Wiley (1964), 93–158.

Fraassen, B. C. van (1995) 'Belief and the Problem of Ulysses and the Sirens', *Philosophical Studies* 77, 7–37.

Gigerenzer, G. et al. (1989) *The Empire of Chance*, Cambridge: Cambridge University Press.

Gillies, D. (2000) *Philosophical Theories of Probability*, London: Routledge.

Glymour, C. (1980) *Theory and Evidence*, Princeton: Princeton University Press.

Goldman, A. (1976) 'Discrimination and Perceptual Knowledge', in *Perceptual Knowledge*, ed. J. Dancy, Oxford: Oxford University Press (1988), 43–65.

Goodman, N. (1965) *Fact, Fiction, and Forecast*, 2nd edn, New York: Bobbs-Merrill.

Grice, H. P. (1961) 'The Causal Theory of Perception', in *Perceptual Knowledge*, ed. J. Dancy, Oxford: Oxford University Press (1988), 66–78.

Hacking, I. (1975) *The Emergence of Probability*, Cambridge: Cambridge University Press.

— (1990) *The Taming of Chance*, Cambridge: Cambridge University Press.

Hájek, A. (2001) 'Probability, Logic and Probability Logic', in *The Blackwell Guide to Philosophical Logic*, ed. L. Goble, Oxford: Blackwell, 362–84.

Howson, C. and Urbach, P. (1993) *Scientific Reasoning: The Bayesian Approach*, 2nd edn, La Salle, Illinois: Open Court.

Hume, D. (1748) 'An Enquiry concerning Human Understanding', in his *Enquiries concerning the Human Understanding and concerning the Principles of Morals*, ed. L. A. Selby-Bigge, Oxford: Clarendon Press (1902), 5–165.

Humphreys, P. (1998) 'Probability, Interpretations of', in *Routledge Encyclopedia of Philosophy*, ed. E. J. Craig, London: Routledge.

Jackson, F., ed. (1991) *Conditionals*, Oxford: Oxford University Press.

Jeffrey, R. C. (1983) *The Logic of Decision*, 2nd edn, Chicago: University of Chicago Press.

— (1985) 'Probability and the Art of Judgment', in his *Probability and the Art of Judgment*, Cambridge: Cambridge University Press (1992), 44–76.

Kahneman, D. and Tversky, A. (1974) 'Judgement under Uncertainty: Heuristics and Biases', in *Judgement under Uncertainty: Heuristics and Biases*, ed. D. Kahneman, P. Slovic and A. Tversky, Cambridge: Cambridge University Press (1982), 3–20.

Kahneman, D., Slovic, P. and Tversky, A., eds (1982) *Judgment Under Uncertainty: Heuristics and Biases*, Cambridge: Cambridge University Press.

Keynes, J. M. (1921) *A Treatise on Probability*, London: Macmillan.

Kirkham, R. L. (1998) 'Truth, Coherence Theory of', in *Routledge Encyclopedia of Philosophy*, ed. E. J. Craig, London: Routledge.

Kneale, W. C. (1949) *Probability and Induction*, Oxford: Clarendon Press.

Kolmogorov, A. N. (1933) *Foundations of the Theory of Probability*, English edn, New York: Chelsea.

Kripke, S. A. (1972) 'Naming and Necessity', in *Semantics of Natural Language*, ed. D. Davidson and G. Harman, Dordrecht: Reidel (1972), 253–355.

— (1980) *Naming and Necessity*, Oxford: Oxford University Press.

Kuipers, T. A. F. (1998) 'Confirmation Theory', in *Routledge Encyclopedia of Philosophy*, ed. E. J. Craig, London: Routledge.

Kyburg, H. E., Jr, ed. (1964) *Studies in Subjective Probability*, New York: Wiley.

— (1970) *Probability and Inductive Logic*, New York: Macmillan.

Laplace, P. S. de (1820) *A Philosophical Essay on Probabilities*, 6th French edn, trans. F. W. Truscott and F. L. Emory, New York: Dover (1951).

Lehrer, K. (1974) *Knowledge*, Oxford: Oxford University Press.

Levi, I. (1980) *The Enterprise of Knowledge*, Cambridge, Mass.: MIT Press.

Lewis, D. K. (1973a) 'Causation', in *Causation*, ed. E. Sosa and M. Tooley, Oxford: Oxford University Press (1993), 193–204.

— (1973b) *Counterfactuals*, Oxford: Blackwell.

— (1973c) 'Possible Worlds', in *The Possible and the Actual*, ed. M. J. Loux, Ithaca: Cornell University Press (1979), 182–9.

— (1976) 'Probabilities of Conditionals and Conditional Probabilities', in his *Philosophical Papers*, vol. II, Oxford: Oxford University Press (1986), 133–56.

— (1980a) 'A Subjectivist's Guide to Objective Chance', in his *Philosophical Papers*, vol. II, Oxford: Oxford University Press (1986), 83–113.

— (1980b) 'Veridical Hallucination and Prosthetic Vision', in *Perceptual Knowledge*, ed. J. Dancy, Oxford: Oxford University Press (1988), 79–91.

— (1983) 'New Work for a Theory of Universals', in *Properties*, ed. D. H. Mellor and A. Oliver, Oxford: Oxford University Press (1997), 188–227.

— (1986) *Philosophical Papers*, vol. II, Oxford: Oxford University Press.

— (1994) 'Humean Supervenience Debugged', *Mind* 103, 473–90.

— (1997) 'Why Conditionalize?' in his *Papers in Metaphysics and Epistemology*, Cambridge: Cambridge University Press (1999), 403–7.

— (1999) *Papers in Metaphysics and Epistemology*, Cambridge: Cambridge University Press.

Loux, M. J., ed. (1979) *The Possible and the Actual*, Ithaca: Cornell University Press.

Luper-Foy, S., ed. (1987) *The Possibility of Knowledge: Nozick and His Critics*, Totowa, NJ: Rowman & Littlefield.

Mackie, J. L. (1974) *The Cement of the Universe*, Oxford: Clarendon Press.

Mellor, D. H. (1971) *The Matter of Chance*, Cambridge: Cambridge University Press.

— (1995) *The Facts of Causation*, London: Routledge.

— (1997) 'Properties and Predicates', in *Properties*, ed. D. H. Mellor and A. Oliver, Oxford: Oxford University Press, 255–67.

— (2000a) 'Possibility, Chance and Necessity', *Australasian Journal of Philosophy* 78, 16–27.

Mellor, D. H., (2000b) 'The Semantics and Ontology of Dispositions', *Mind* 109, 757–80.

Mellor, D. H. and Oliver, A., eds (1997) *Properties*, Oxford: Oxford University Press.

Miller, D., ed. (1983) *The Pocket Popper*, London: Fontana.

Mises, R. von (1957) *Probability, Statistics and Truth*, 2nd English edn, London: Allen & Unwin.

Moser, P. K., ed. (1990) *Rationality in Action*, Cambridge: Cambridge University Press.

Mumford, S. (1998) *Dispositions*, Oxford: Oxford University Press.

Nozick, R. (1981a) 'Knowledge and Scepticism', in *Perceptual Knowledge*, ed. J. Dancy, Oxford: Oxford University Press (1988), 21–42.

— (1981b) *Philosophical Explanations*, Oxford: Oxford University Press.

Plantinga, A. (1976) 'Actualism and Possible Worlds', in *The Possible and the Actual*, ed. M. J. Loux, Ithaca: Cornell University Press (1979), 253–73.

Plato, J. von (1994) *Creating Modern Probability*, Cambridge: Cambridge University Press.

Popper, K. R. (1957) 'The Propensity Interpretation of the Calculus of Probability, and the Quantum Theory', in *Observation and Interpretation in the Philosophy of Physics*, ed. S. Körner, London: Butterworth, 65–70.

— (1990) *A World of Propensities*, Bristol: Thoemmes.

Ramsey, F. P. (1926) 'Truth and Probability', in his *Philosophical Papers*, ed. D. H. Mellor, Cambridge: Cambridge University Press (1990), 52–109.

Reichenbach, H. (1949) *The Theory of Probability*, Berkeley: University of California Press.

Russell, B. (1948) *Human Knowledge: Its Scope and Limits*, London: Allen & Unwin.

Ryle, G. (1949) *The Concept of Mind*, London: Hutchinson.

Salmon, W. C. (1980) 'Probabilistic Causality', in *Causation*, ed. E. Sosa and M. Tooley, Oxford: Oxford University Press (1993), 137–53.

— (1990) 'Rationality and Objectivity in Science *or* Tom Kuhn Meets Tom Bayes', in *The Philosophy of Science*, ed. D. Papineau, Oxford: Oxford University Press (1996), 256–89.

Shoemaker, S. (1980) 'Causality and Properties', in *Properties*, ed. D. H. Mellor and A. Oliver, Oxford: Oxford University Press (1997), 228–54.

Sklar, L. (1992) *Philosophy of Physics*, Boulder, Colo.: Westview Press.

— (1993) *Physics and Chance: Philosophical Issues in the Foundations of Statistical Mechanics*, New York: Cambridge University Press.

Skyrms, B. (1980) *Causal Necessity*, New Haven: Yale University Press.

Sosa, E. and Tooley, M., eds (1993) *Causation*, Oxford: Oxford University Press.

Stalnaker, R. C. (1976) 'Possible Worlds', in *The Possible and the Actual*, ed. M. J. Loux, Ithaca: Cornell University Press (1979), 225–34.

Swinburne, R. G., ed. (2002) *Bayes's Theorem*, Oxford: Oxford University Press.

Teller, P. (1973) 'Conditionalisation and Observation', *Synthese* 26, 218–58.

Tooley, M. (1987) *Causation: a Realist Approach*, Oxford: Clarendon Press.

Tversky, A. and Kahneman, D. (1982) 'Evidential Impact of Base Rates', in *Judgment Under Uncertainty: Heuristics and Biases*, ed. D. Kahneman, P. Slovic and A. Tversky, Cambridge: Cambridge University Press, 153–60.

Venn, J. (1888) 'The Subjective Side of Probability', in *Studies in Subjective Probability*, ed. H. E. Kyburg, Jr and H. E. Smokler, New York: Wiley (1964), 17–43.

Walker, R. C. S. (1989) *The Coherence Conception of Truth*, London: Routledge.

Index

temperature 12, 23, 46, 59, 67–8, 74,
77, 133
tendencies 49–51
testimony 11, 102, 124
theoretical entities 141
theoretical idealisation 71
theory-ladenness 101
Tooley, M. 44
total evidence principle 81, 124
Tversky, A. 122–6
ultimate possibilities 4, 24–6, 29, 39,
45–7

uncertainty 2, 65, 77
utilities
expected subjective. *See* expected
subjective utility
subjective 12, 75–7, 80, 116

Venn, J. 78

Walker, R. C. S. 111
wishful thinking 102–4